On this poet's garden tour, Sarah Salway writes of the gardens' physical selves, of course, but also of the sensations they conjure, the memories they stir up and the glimpses of history that colour her perception. Each description is rich, layered, personal and moving. It is more like the way we all experience gardens than any garden writing I have come across.

Sarah has a unique combination of a garden lover's eye and a poet's imagination, and it is a delicious treat to watch her exercise them on this group of gardens. She makes a fascinating and unpredictable virtual garden companion, always drawing your attention to some unexpected detail, or taking some half-told story, exploring it and breaking your heart with it. At the end I desperately wanted to set her onto my own favourite gardens and see what happens.

I read this book sometimes with a silly smile on my face, sometimes gripped and anxious, often with a tingle running down my spine. Sarah's poetry has always moved me, and now she writes about my favourite subject, gardens. How lucky we gardeners are to have her in our midst. This could not be a lovelier book.

Lia Leendertz, who writes about gardens for
The Guardian, The Daily Telegraph and others

In *Digging up Paradise* Sarah Salway has drawn thoughtful and imaginative pathways for the reader through the horticultural persons, places and histories of Kent. Through an arboretum of writing these spaces come alive on the page, providing a moment of instant verdant escape for the committed armchair traveller.

Part-travelogue, part-poetry collection, part-guide-book, *Digging up Paradise* moves from landscaped castle grounds to shell grottoes, from desolate public parks to topiaried views, gathering creative seeds and espaliering the stories so that a sense of each place can be quickly understood and enjoyed. Reading this book has inspired me to take my own notebook out into my local green patches, and left me with hopeful plans to visit the Garden of England that these 'cuttings' make sound so enticing.

Viccy Adams, Writer and Literary Artist

Sarah Salway's new collection is an original and engaging take on a perennial theme – pun intended! Gardens have occupied the imaginations of poets for generations, from Hafiz writing in ancient Persia to Rudyard Kipling declaring that 'All England is a garden'. In moving, engaging and often surprising reflections, Sarah Salway takes the reader on a tour of the Garden of England, introducing us to the stories of Kent's astonishing variety of well-known and tucked-away gardens. As we'd expect from this widely praised and published writer, her prose is expansive and generous and the poems distilled and precise. As a bonus, both are illustrated by Sarah Salway's own photographs. This is a book to treasure and to carry on summer picnics to these captivating and ever-changing oases – a worthy paean to gardens and the gardeners who created them.

Victoria Field, author of *The Lost Boys*

This remarkable creation – part guided tour, part literary and history essay, part poetry – is rich testament to Salway's entirely passionate and insightful observations as a writer and self-confessed, lifelong biophile.

In *Digging Up Paradise,* Salway charts interior and exterior journeys as she travels through Kent's gardens. From Margate Shell Grotto to Sissinghurst Castle, we travel with her via an eclectic mixture of photos, journal entries, and exquisite poems, often to our own real and remembered gardens, and the people in them. This book surprises and delights us with what we never knew, or knew and had forgotten, reconnecting us with our own public and private spaces. With characteristic lightness of touch and lively enquiry, Salway explores our relationships with the natural world: how we live and create in it, and how it lives and breathes in us.

Patricia Debney, author of *Littoral* and *How to Be a Dragonfly*

Sarah Salway is a novelist and poet living in Kent. She grew up surrounded by gardens as the daughter of garden historian and writer, Elizabeth Peplow, and is now a full member of the Garden Media Guild. Sarah is the recipient of Fellowships from Hawthornden in Scotland, the VCCA in the USA, and was the Royal Literature Fund Fellow at the London School of Economics and Political Science. This book started during her term as Canterbury Laureate, and more gardens and photographs can be found on her website, www.writerinthegarden.com.

Acknowledgements

The author and publisher are grateful to the garden owners for permission to use the author's photographs of the gardens in this book.

Without the following people, this garden journey wouldn't have been so interesting or so much fun. I'm grateful to them all for their enthusiasm for the project, good advice and generous sharing of wisdom:

Alison Chambers and the Canterbury Festival; Beth Cuenco and the Wise Words team; Viccy Adams; Kim Addonizio; Will Sutton; S.J. Butler; Patricia Debney; Victoria Field; Lia Leendertz; Michelle Lovric; Gregory Warren Wilson; Danuta Kean; Anne Kelly; Alice Elliott Dark; Veryan Pendarves; Katie Campbell; Catherine Smith; Gaye Jee; Anna Lambert; Clare Law; Pamela Johnson; Rachael Hale; Gaynor Edwards; Ellen Montelius; Mark Holihan; Stephanie Decouvelaere; Maria C. McCarthy and Bob Carling of Cultured Llama, and of course to the gardeners, curators and owners of the beautiful gardens of Kent.

But most of all to Francis, Hugh and Rachael who have had to put up with a lot of 'garden-talk' over the years.

Digging Up Paradise:
Potatoes, People and Poetry in the Garden of England

Previous books by Sarah Salway

Novels
Tell Me Everything (2011)
Getting the Picture (2010)
Something Beginning With (2005)

Short Stories
Leading the Dance (2011)

Poetry
You Do Not Need Another Self-Help Book (2012)

Digging Up Paradise:
Potatoes, People and Poetry in the Garden of England

Sarah Salway

For Brenda,
With best wishes,
Sarah Salway
June 2014

First published in 2014 by
Cultured Llama Publishing
11 London Road
Teynham, Sittingbourne
ME9 9QW
www.culturedllama.co.uk

The right of Sarah Salway to be identified as the author of this work has been asserted by her in accordance with Section 77 of the Copyright, Designs and Patents Act 1988

A CIP record for this book is available from The British Library

ISBN 978-0-9926485-6-5

Printed in Great Britain by Lightning Source UK Ltd

Jacket design by Mark Holihan
Interior design by Bob Carling
Map by Ellen Montelius
Copy editing by Stephanie Decouvelaere
All photos by Sarah Salway

Contents

'Now there,' said he, pointing his finger, 'I make a comma, and there,' pointing to another spot, 'where a more decided turn is proper, I make a colon; at another part, where an interruption is desirable to break the view, a parenthesis; now a full stop, and then I begin another subject.'

Lancelot 'Capability' Brown describes how he
designs a garden to Mrs Hannah Moore

Letter to a Stranger, a Homegrown project in Greyfriars Garden, Canterbury, 2012

Dear Stranger

What would *you* say if you were writing to a stranger? And where would you like to be writing – and reading – that letter?

What about a quiet garden only just yards away from Canterbury's busy High Street? One that you enter through wooden gates after following a path Chaucer's pilgrims may have taken over not just one simple bridge but two, because this garden sits in the fork of the river, fed on both sides by the Stour. Add a chapel that was consecrated in the 13th Century when St Francis of Assisi was still alive, and which sits in a field of wild flowers circled by a mown lawn path.

This is Greyfriars Garden in Canterbury and when, as Canterbury Laureate in 2012, I was invited to stage an 'intervention' here, I knew I wanted to work with the three qualities I had experienced in the garden. The first was how quiet it is. So peaceful in fact, that I always have to stand still to work out what it is I'm not hearing: traffic noise, other people, machinery. Second, a sense of safety helped by the old walls and river inlets that hold this garden as if welcoming deep thoughts of past, present and future. And lastly, the contrast in atmosphere between the frenzy of the nearby shopping street and this space where I don't have to do anything, be anything, buy anything. I can sit alone but not feel lonely. So, during the Wise Words Festival and working with the Reauthoring Project, I set up a little stall in the garden, picked postcards from my own collection and invited people into the garden to write a message to a stranger. These were then pinned up on makeshift 'washing lines' hung around the garden for everybody to browse until they found the card they wanted to take home.

We had poetry, confessions, messages of love and encouragement, angry stories, sad stories, inspiring quotes, jokes and invitations to talk further. At least one friendship resulted from two strangers connecting through these postcards, and as one writer said: 'They say all art is stealing but that doesn't feel quite right because Canterbury today is giving me this feeling, this feeling I'm going to be thinking about today all night.'

And it's right that these 'feelings' can and should happen in gardens – places of alchemy where we can make our own boundaries to turn a public space into our own private paradise. There's even a word for it – biophilia – which means a connection, a love or an ease with one's natural surroundings.

I know all about this because I've used public gardens as my own at different times in my life. When I first left home to live in a London flat, I missed the countryside so much that I'd take my shoes off in my local park so I could remind myself there was grass and earth under all that concrete. Lonely and a little bit frightened, I would often write in my journal about the other park users and what I imagined their lives to be. Then, in Edinburgh, when my children were small, we had a key to one of the city's garden squares that my son called 'the country'. We'd take picnics so he could run around enough to tire himself out, and he held his first birthday party there. And now, I live in the middle of higgledy-piggledy Tunbridge Wells, where our 'patio' is so open to the cobbled street that our predecessors once came back to some tourists enjoying their sandwiches at the garden table. Perhaps it's not surprising that I escape to our local common as often as I can to breathe in the trees and reconnect with grass.

I'm sure it's a hangover from my childhood when my garden historian mother, Elizabeth Peplow, opened the herb gardens she'd designed to the public. I got used to keeping corners of the garden for myself, watching in turn how visitors would often treat 'my' garden as their own.

These boundaries between private spaces and public grounds were the seeds that grew into what became first the *Writer In The Garden* website (www. writerinthegarden.com) and then this book. Canterbury being the heart of Kent, and Kent being the Garden of England, I made my Laureate project a creative exploration of public gardens in Kent. I thought I'd be exploring typically English gardens, but what quickly transpired was that this book actually contains very little that is strictly English. Plants, trees, designs, planting styles have come from all over the world to flourish together in what could be chaos but ends up alive and vibrant. 'He who plants a garden plants happiness,' the saying goes, and just as people make the difference between a building and a home, so they turn a landscape into a garden.

So this is a book about gardens, but mostly it is about people. The strangers whose footsteps I've followed through the gardens and whom I have come to know – three asthmatic brothers who built a formal garden together as the world stood poised on the edge of war; a thirteen-year-old boy sentenced for stealing roses in the 19th Century; a man obsessed with building his own ruins; artists of perspective; hornpipe dancers; plant collectors; apple scrumpers.

There are twenty-six gardens here to make up a horticultural alphabet, and although there is a map which suggests a tour, this isn't only a guide book or even a book stuffed full of gardening advice or history. It is a book you might take into a garden to read and dream a little of who sat there before you. But I hope too that you will put it down to write your own letter to a stranger and leave it in the garden for someone to find. There are a few writing 'seeds' hidden in here to provide inspiration.

Sarah Salway

A view to the Cathedral from
Greyfriars Garden, Canterbury

Letter to a Stranger

Last night I dreamt of a blue plate
piled high with strawberry-shaped words.
Trust. Kind. You. Flourish.
This morning I followed the path
round a green bowl filled with wildflowers.

Look, I want to say,
so much has gone before us,
so much will happen next,
not every day needs a destination
or to make sense.

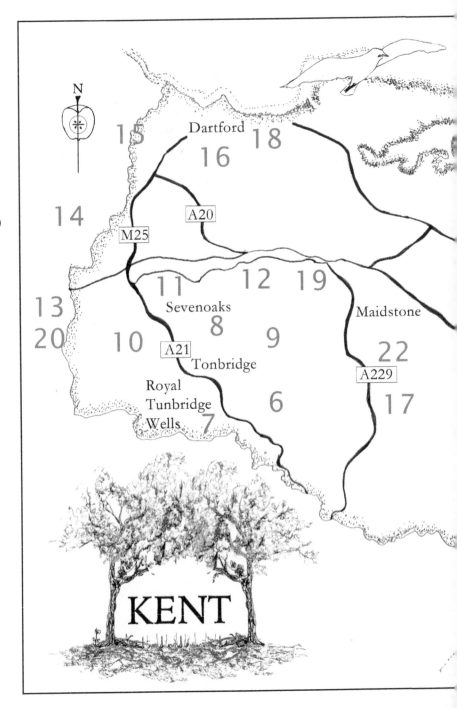

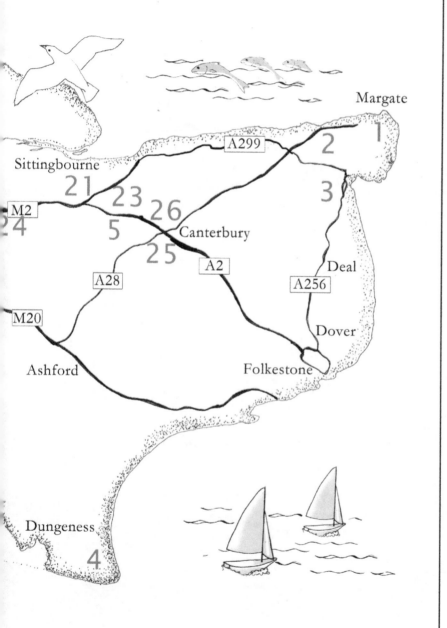

Map by Ellen Montelius

The shell grotto,
Margate

1 The Shell Grotto, Margate

Imagine this: it's 1835 and you are Joshua Newlove, a small boy proudly watching your father dig a duck pond in your back garden in Margate. But something's wrong. The spade goes in so deep that it seems to fall into the ground. When your father asks you to go down the hole to investigate what's happened, you don't hesitate. You love adventure, but even you aren't prepared for what you'll find. You come back wide-eyed with stories of magic passages, of mermaid's palaces, of tunnels lined with treasures from the sea. What will, in fact, turn out to be two thousand square feet of shell mosaics.

How the Margate Shell Grotto was discovered by the Newlove family is only part of its legend. Grottos have always been important, and often magical, garden jewels and Margate's mysterious shell grotto is no exception. The fact that the genesis of this grotto still remains a delicious mystery adds to its drama. Over the years since it was discovered, experts and enthusiasts have come up with different theories as to who built it, from the Phoenicians to Victorians to smugglers to opportunistic businessmen to two young brothers playing in the 1800s. The fumes from the gaslights used in Victorian times polluted the shells and mean that carbon dating can't be used.

After its discovery, it became a fashionable place to visit. The Victorian novelist Marie Corelli said, 'If the curious and beautiful subterranean temple existed anywhere but Margate, it would certainly be acknowledged as one of the wonders of the world.' In the 1930s and 40s there were some famous séances held in the grotto, and the marvellously named guide book *Far From the Sodding Crowd*, by Jason Hazeley, Robin Halstead, Alex Morris and Joel Morrison, states: 'In the next six months, unless your soul is utterly dead, you will have a dream set here.'

Dreams aside, to get to the grotto you have to leave the sea-front and walk up the suburban streets until you reach a perfectly unremarkable residential street, apart from one giveaway clue: it's called Grotto Hill. Then you go through the kind of gift shop you might find in any seaside town selling postcards, rocks and children's shell jewellery. Once you've purchased your ticket, you go down – and down – a sandy path to find yourself in this labyrinth of shells, over four million of them. I quickly realised that either I could go mad trying to work out the truth, or I could give myself up to the winding, dancing, swirling, unexpected magic of the place. It felt feminine. It felt as if I was dancing. It felt as if I was entering a conversation. It felt as if I could shut my eyes and wish for whatever I wanted – there is apparently a wishing shell here: find it and press on it and your dreams will come true.

I didn't find the wishing shell, but Sarah Vickery, the current owner of the grotto, made me wait (rather nervously) in one spot as she went to stand next to the whispering shells. Although she was too far away for me to see her, her whispers echoed loudly round the chamber. The walls of the chambers and passages are decorated by pointed arches of shells, mostly in geometrical designs of stars, diamonds and flower arrangements. The shells are mostly whelk, oysters and dog-winkle, and are smoked a rich brown from the gas lights, which seems to add to the mystery.

I surprised myself by the poem I wrote for the Grotto. It's much more personal than my other garden poems, and yet all the things I was noticing – a conversation, the labyrinthine tunnels, birth, skeletons – are in here. The amazing mystery of creation.

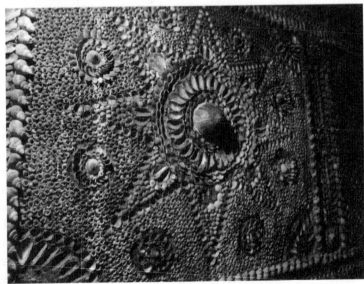

A detail from a shell panel

Mystery

I told everyone I didn't care,
so long as it's healthy,
but sitting on a bus one day
watching mothers and daughters turn
in to one another,
(how did I even know the relationship?)
I had to stroke my stomach,
every finger an appeal, and later,

when I held you through that first night,
tiny body settled in the crook of my arm,
I'd have turned myself inside out
to give you my skeleton as protection;
we stared at each other, our conversation
begun long before either of us was born
and though I wanted to tell every happy
ending, could only whisper, *you,*

into that shell-like ear, had to trust
you to find the tunnel that led past
the talking wall to find the one wishing
shell, and on to the ray of light
falling like a perfect circle in your path,
and the fact that you didn't know
how you'd got there, or even your purpose,
is your mystery to unravel, not mine.

A tree found at
Quex Gardens

2 Quex Gardens, Birchington

There's a certain historic khaki-shorted, fine-moustached Englishman I always get a crush on. I wouldn't want to marry one though, not least because they usually had one failing: big game hunting. Instead of flowers, they'd bring you animal skins, filling the house with rugs or taxidermy specimens.

Chief amongst these must have been Major Percy Powell-Cotton, owner of Quex House until 1940. There's a story that sums him up for me: when he was out in Africa at the beginning of the 1900s, he was saved from being fatally injured by a lion by the rolled up copy of *Punch* magazine in his top pocket, which protected his heart from the lion's claws. After this, I expect he carried on with the rest of his day as if nothing had happened; he certainly had his revenge on the lion, as it's now part of an extraordinary exhibition of animal dioramas you visit at the house. These are still so well maintained, the taxidermy so skilful and the backgrounds painted so vividly that scientific and zoology scholars continue to come from all over the world.

There are several ways to visit a garden. One is by knowing the history before, both socially and botanically; another is by surrendering to emotional senses, and yet another is trusting to serendipity. The truth is that I went to Quex on that particular day after I picked up a leaflet at the Margate Shell Grotto and realised how close I was, so, by default, my visit fell into the last two categories.

When I walked round the garden for the first time I couldn't help feeling that despite its beauty, there was an underlying layer of sadness. It was spring, and I could admire the tulips and primroses, the roses about to burst into bud and the exotic trees. The walled vegetable garden was full of promise and the house loomed theatrically across the circular pond from the wild woodland mound at the edge of the grounds. It had been raining and the whole garden was as languid and full as if it had just got out of a hot bath, but I felt I'd been hit by an emotional wave.

Above the flower beds, I noticed how a chain link had become ingrown into a tree trunk, the geraniums looked as if they were trying to escape from the greenhouse, and even the benches invited me to sit down and have a little weep.

Ridiculous?

I have a sneaking suspicion Major Percy would think so, but when I read the history of the gardens, I found that during The First World War, Major and Mrs Powell-Cotton had offered up their house as a military hospital. Expecting British officers, they were surprised to find injured soldiers from Belgium, many not speaking a word of English, waiting for them at the local train station. There were so many more soldiers than promised that they were forced to put up temporary beds in the exhibition rooms, and the next morning the invalids woke up next to an array of pouncing stuffed animals before the dioramas were swiftly covered over with sheets.

Despite this, it seems that many of the patients thrived at Quex, working in the garden as part of their convalescence. In fact the vegetable garden became so productive that the war office wrote to complain that the Powell-Cottons were giving the patients too much food. There are accounts of soldiers painting African backdrops to the dioramas, walking up to the Wellington memorial and looking after Major Percy's collection of cannons. Mrs Powell-Cotton turned out to be a natural nurse, and was joined by friends including the Australian novelist, Margaret Mary Marlowe, who arrived for a week's trial and stayed for the duration.

The soldiers' stories stayed with me as I walked round the grounds after finding out about this particular bit of Quex's history and I could feel how therapeutic a garden like this must have been. The story of one soldier, Camille, resonated in particular. Although he didn't speak one word for the two years he was in England, he started talking the minute he set foot on his home soil in Belgium.

A detail from one of the statues at Quex Gardens

Letter to Camille

You could speak if you wanted to, but the words are stuck in your heart when they should flow through your veins. You don't have the words for what you've seen, even the letters that make up the words are weapons because if such things exist then they could happen again.

Dam. Age. Damn this age of ours.

Because it's true the enemy must be a boy like you, who dreams at night of a father's hand over his on the spade, or a mother's private smile as she hands him the first ripe tomato to smell and then, *go on, no one is looking,* to taste. It's true the enemy was once a boy for whom the very word, Africa, spelt adventure but he could also be your friend who faints the first morning when the screen is pulled back and he sees he's been sleeping next to a lion. He's next to you now as you stare at the animals during Major Percy's show-and-tell. He's your friend painting the backdrop for a giraffe to walk across, the two of you gambling over cards in the evening, climbing up to the tower together, arguing over which of Major Percy Powell-Cotton's collection of cannons would fire the furthest. Blushing as he's caught staring a little too long at Major Percy's English wife.

In-ger-land. Kut.

They catch you one morning, your hand on the bark of a tree. St-uck. But what they don't know is you can feel the sap rising, how the tree is drawing its own strength from the earth. Trreee. You shake your head, put your hand up to pull a leaf down, point to the edges as clumsily cut as if by a child. Oak. You nod.

9

Oak. Grass. Bud. Flower. Weed.

They think they're just teaching you English, but you know the truth. You are building a wall of words inside, a cover to keep you safe until.

Australia.

You've looked it up on an old map in the museum. One day you're walking beside her as she wheels the medicine trolley round the wards when she suddenly takes off.

Gee-whiz!

She's through the door and over the patio and out on to the lawn. The trolley's wheels making marks like directions on the grass, and you're following because you like the idea of creating a new map.

The space in my country, she says, *you can breathe better in it. Sometimes I just need air,* and then shockingly, surprisingly, she folds herself over to stand on her hands, a waterfall of white petticoat, a glimpse that shudders you down to your feet until you're not sure you're not upside down too. But then she's upright, and somehow you are too. *Ah,* she says, as she moulds herself back to the medicine trolley and leaves you so smoothly, you'd swear she was moving on wheels too if you hadn't seen. Surely you did see.

Ah, she says over her shoulder, *he might not talk but he can sigh,* and before you know it, you laugh.

Then you remember.

Fresh air and brisk walks, Major Powell-Cotton says. *Good food and kindness,* Mrs Powell-Cotton says. *Clean bandages and rest,* the nurses say. *Hard work and a clean mind,* your mother always said. But still you say nothing.

Until one day, you look around and see things as they are. There are no soldiers creeping through the woods.

No blood in the grass.

The trees aren't caged.

And the bark doesn't leak poison.

Chimneys are just there to heat the greenhouses and to nurture the plants.

That's how you know the news. Even before Major Powell-Cotton comes across the lawn to find you, each cheer you hear echoing through the space behind him is like a series of flags being hoisted. Home, you whisper, and you don't care that no one hears because the word bangs round your head until you wonder if all of the Quex cannons have been fired at the same time. You're off.

Home. Home. Home.

The House of Salutation,
Secret Gardens of Sandwich

3 The Secret Gardens of Sandwich

A Change of Air

You'd be sure to notice the gasworks first,
worry how close the garden sits,
until you learn this is why it was built,

three wheezing brothers filling
their lungs with sea salt and gas fumes:
the latest thing in London, Lutyens

also, while from over the sea
the smooth sounds of bandstands,
tea cups clinking in pre-war courtyards,

imagine three garden chairs lined up
to face smoking chimneys, a sound of gasping,
bad static waiting to be tuned,

so many farewells hanging in the balance,
a world struggling to catch its breath.

At the time of writing this, the Secret Gardens of Sandwich are recovering from recent devastating floods when the garden was covered by several feet of salt water. Although many of the plants are feared to be lost for good and thousands of pounds of damage has been done, the gardens are open again. It is a reminder of how tenuous gardens can be, because when I first visited here in 2011, the then owner, Dominic Parker, was showing me how he had brought the garden back to life after moving there in 2004.

It's always a different experience walking round a garden with either the owner, gardener or, as Dominic prefers to call it, custodian. Instead of being left alone with your own thoughts, you walk forward ten paces, wait for him or her to stoop down to pick a weed or admire a plant that's doing particularly well, and then you walk another ten paces, stop and do the whole thing all over again. And again.

Because I didn't particularly enjoy growing up in a house with a garden open to the public, I was interested that Dominic so obviously loved having visitors. His fa-

A corner of the Secret Gardens of Sandwich

vourite visitor, he said, was a season-ticket holder who sat in exactly the same spot every day to knit. After watching her for a time, he thought he'd better say hello, but apparently she'd looked up in complete dismay because it was obviously her garden, not his, for the hour she sat there. He had disturbed her peace.

The house was designed by Edwin Lutyens in 1911 and the gardens are influenced by the work of garden designer, Gertrude Jeckyll. The garden isn't big but is full of detail: a vegetable garden is near the centre rather than being shunted out of sight, a pond with a wooden bridge over to a small island, a white garden that Dominic assures me is earlier than the more famous one at Sissinghurst. There are some architectural patterns in the garden that are pure Lutyens; for instance the little lawn outside the dining room is exactly the same size and proportion as the room inside. It's the sort of thing you wouldn't know unless it was pointed out, and yet the sense of order feels strangely satisfying.

We had one hairy moment when I asked to see the famous Wollemi Pine. This special tree dates back 90 million years, and was only known through fossil records until specimens were rediscovered in 1994 in the rainforest wilderness of the Wollemi National Park in New Zealand. They are still incredibly rare, so I was excited to see a real one.

But it wasn't there.

I had brief visions of it tiptoeing off on spindly roots back to the rainforest until it turned out that the gardeners had moved it to the warmth of the greenhouse.

The original owners of the house (which is splendidly named The House of Salutation) were three unmarried brothers from London, the Farrars, who were looking for a country retreat and commissioned Lutyens to design them one in 1911.

When I was looking at old maps of Sandwich, I was annoyed to see how close the gasworks were built to the gardens; it seemed such an intrusion. However, it turned out that the opposite was true, and the gasworks were the very reason the house was built in that particular spot. The Farrar brothers were asthmatic, and at that time, it was thought that a combination of sea air and gas fumes was the ideal cure.

A detail of Derek Jarman's garden,
Prospect House, Dungeness

4   Dungeness

Is Dungeness a garden?

Years ago, the question of what a garden actually was nearly brought my normally friendly garden history class to fisticuffs. Some students were determined that it had to have the intention of being a private sanctuary, others that it was merely a place that had been cultivated. Most of us agreed that it needed to have some kind of enclosure separating it from the rest of the landscape.

Well, Dungeness blows that particular theory apart.

One of the most famous British modern gardens has to be the one the artist and film director, Derek Jarman, built at Dungeness in the last years of his life. And Prospect House certainly isn't enclosed. Although there are naturalised plants, the main structure is not horticulturally based, consisting instead of beautiful stones and driftwood. You get the feeling that whatever plant chooses to grow in such a gorgeously desolate spot will be welcome.

But it is definitely still a garden if you believe that gardens can be composed as much of feelings and emotions, of glooms and sunspots, as they can of flowers and trees. A garden is more of a process than an object, and Dungeness is unique because of its elements of domestication in the middle of pure wildness. I'm not sure if it's out of either choice or necessity but those who live there don't seem to impose their wishes on the landscape. Even the white picket fence around one particular garden looks ironic.

It's certainly a place of contrasts. A nuclear power station next to a national nature reserve. A bleak landscape that has just recorded a nest of a previously extinct bee, the short-haired bumblebee. The plastic fishing gnome in front of a rickety sea shack. A peculiarly English setting for a war memorial to two Polish Fighter Pilots, Boguslaw Mierzwa and Mieczyslaw Waskiewicz. The loss of two young men is made all the more poignant because they died not in enemy action, but when their spitfires collided with each other over Dungeness on 16 April 1941. Even the aggressively named Viper's Bugloss, with its tall blue flowers, was shaking in the wind like a lesson in how a plant can surrender to its fate better than most humans will ever be able to.

What I also noticed was the paths, leading out to the sea and back to the land. Sometimes these were man-made, sometimes they were found paths – a line of rope that must have been left by a fisherman and which looked as if it wanted to be followed, paths to houses, a straight line of shingle left by the tide.

It's impossible not to feel wild emotion everywhere at Dungeness; I wasn't the only visitor to stand and drink in the sea as if the raw desolation was stilling something inside me. Perhaps it's a prime example of how we need nature to shock us out of the prisons we make in our own minds.

A path out to the sea at Dungeness

That Path to the Sea

Let's build a path like a woman's spine;
we'll keep eyes closed to feel our soles,
the spring in our heels,
put down grass, and sand, sheepskin,
smooth oak, and cashmere,
until no one knows what's coming next,
a line of feathers
so thick it'll feel like floating,
warm wool giving under toes,
steel girders, resin, piano keys.
We know how it will hold us up,
however heavy we are with sadness,
it will hold us up.

The tiered garden at the
back of Chilham Castle

5   Chilham Castle, Chilham

Dawn

And as the garden sleeps,
held safe by Colebrooke's wall,
the straight silvered arrow
of a fox stalks the terraces,

negotiating by ancient impulse
dew embroidered footprints,
until a shift of the earth,
a tremor so slight everything stills.

Morning, the castle's windows
open on a world righted back on itself,
sun rising and setting in a perfect line,
the promise of each day correct and waiting.

Although Chilham Castle is right in the middle of the village, the studded and speared gates are normally shut, so when they opened up for me it felt as if I was entering a film set. The magic was helped by visiting on a misty day so the Castle loomed up ahead.

I was lucky enough to be taken around by Michael Peters, the castle's archivist for the owners, Tessa and Stuart Wheeler. As the ground squeaked with frost under our feet, we discussed the vexing question of whether there were really elephants at Chilham. Elephants had been used for rolling out lawns in other parts of Kent, and the rumour that they were at Chilham is encouraged by a house in the village called the Elephant House. Sadly no evidence has been found ... yet.

Michael is a natural storyteller, and there are so many stories to think about when walking round the garden here, such as the wisteria climbing up the cor-

ner wall, which is supposedly a direct descendant of England's first wisteria brought from China by a certain Captain Robert Wellbank, a family friend of the then owners. Then there was the 'fantasy' cricket match that took place between the visiting national Australian team and 'Mr Wilsher's Gentlemen'.

Even so, the gardens at Chilham Castle offer a feeling of order and pattern, and it wasn't too surprising to find that one avenue of Sweet Chestnut trees has been planted in alignment with the rising sun, and that two yew trees have been discovered - past the grounds and even past the village

Possible descendent of the first wisteria in England

– to follow the line completely. They follow the prehistoric tracks now called the Pilgrim's Way.

Here's what Michael writes about it:

> *The eastern one, known as the Chestnut Avenue, points straight to the courtyard at the heart of the house, where it meets another axis running straight across the village square and into the churchyard where it glances the stump of the ancient yew tree. The symbolism behind this geometry is now a matter for speculation but the orientation of the house and the Chestnut Avenue (with its companion avenue to the west described below) do relate closely to celestial motions – perhaps an echo of the astronomical interests of Sir Dudley's father and grandfather.*

Further order was imposed when the grounds were controversially enclosed in the 1730s by the then owner, James Colebrooke. He lowered the boundary wall by 80 yards, enclosed an area of 80 roods, and is supposed to have changed the course of the River Stour to bring it within 880 yards of the Castle's top terrace. It's a reminder of how geometrical gardening was a craze in the Georgian period, before being largely replaced by the 'natural' lines followed by gardeners such as Capability Brown.

Perhaps it is the fragility of the creation of a garden – having to contend with soil, weather, elements – that makes gardeners so obsessive about structure. Gardens can never be stable in time like other artworks, so it was interesting to look over Chilham's tiered garden with its precisely maintained topiary bushes to the rolling fields of Kent beyond and remember how the philanthropist John Paul Getty purchased the land directly around Ely Cathedral so that the view could be preserved for ever. Lovely to think of a view as important as any painting.

A garden piano
at Finchcocks

6 Finchcocks Musical Museum, Goudhurst

'm not sure why walking in the garden of this Georgian Manor House just outside Tunbridge Wells feels as if you have stepped into another time.

Perhaps it's because every wall seems to have a doorway you go through to find something unexpected on the other side: two geese and a duck, a tumble of white roses, a wooden case of a green-painted piano with a stool inviting you to sit down, a sign to the 'Enchanted Compost Heap'. And then round every corner, I stumbled on something from the past: an abandoned grass roller, a pink and purple sedan chair, apple boxes.

Maybe it is because the whole garden feels as if it is just on the cusp of falling over into abandonment, albeit in the best possible way because I should point out these thirteen acres have been fully restored. However, the romance remains, a very different feeling from the more formal gardens I visited.

It's said about violins that certain vibrations made over years can make microscopic changes in the wood. The instrument therefore remembers its players, and the garden at Finchcocks gives the feeling of remembering its gardeners. I wouldn't have been surprised to come across gardeners from the past tying up the white climbing roses or sitting having a cup of tea. Perhaps even the hum of an old song in the air, as I noticed a clump of foxgloves with their mouths open wide as if about to burst into song.

I had a sudden memory of the time my father took me – as a child – to hear Vivaldi's *The Four Seasons* in London. I've never forgotten how much he laughed when I jumped during the summer thunderstorm. In fact, he laughed so hard he was asked to hush by someone in the row behind us. A fact that went a little way to making up for my own humiliation.

It's certainly true that there is a musical theme going on here. Not surprising because the house is a musical museum with a famous collection of instruments you can visit. In fact, they are almost celebrities in their own right, with instruments featuring in films such as *Pride and Prejudice, Sense and Sensibility* and *Vanity Fair*, amongst many others. There are regular recitals at Finchcocks every Sunday, where for the price of your entry ticket, you can combine your garden visit with listening to world-class musicians play to you in rooms that make you feel you are in your own Jane Austen novel.

One instrument in the collection I can't stop thinking about is the harpsichord, which has been specially built so the music can only be heard by the person playing it.

I took this thought with me into the garden afterwards as I sat on a bench against one of the ivy coloured walls and watched the light making silent songs with shadows on the grass.

One of the many 'magic' doorways at Finchcocks

My Father Always Liked Loud Noises

I should have known something was up
when the trip was first announced –
A classical concert, us?
I sat shredding the frills
on my new stiff petticoat,
running my nails the wrong way
across red velvet seats –
stop fidgeting – until
musicians filed on stage, one by one,
how many could there be? – *stop yawning* –
then a conductor summoned images like magic,
his baton swaying wand-like and I was cut
in half, made whole, half, whole,
pulled from a dozen top hats,
a coloured dove flying high,
five hundred silk scarves floating free,
icy rain and hot sun,
until my father took my hand in his,
I squeezed back – *thank you* – until
BOOM –
I turned to see his shoulders shaking
'you jumped!' but the truth was
I'd been wound up like spring
since the very first note.

A view of the house from the
formal garden, Groombridge Place

7 Groombridge Place, Groombridge

Even if you have never been to Groombridge Place, you'd probably recognise it straight away.

Albeit under a different name. Compton Anstey, perhaps, in Peter Greenaway's film *The Draughtsman's Contract* where the stunning Tudor garden was the model for Mr Neville, the draughtsman, to paint his twelve portraits. Then it's also Longbourne Manor, the Bennet's slightly rundown home in Joe Wright's *Pride and Prejudice*. And on the page, it's been Birlstone Manor in the Sherlock Holmes story, *The Valley of Fear*.

So when you drive past the moated house to reach the public entrance at the back, it already feels a bit starry. And also, let's be honest, slightly decadent and sexy. Or half of it does anyway. Because, this is a garden of two halves.

One half is the 'theme park' side to Groom-bridge Place – the boat ride, the piglet racing, mirrored

The 'Mystic garden'

garden, bone-shaped benches, adventure playground and Romany caravans. All good fun. I'm a sucker for these parts of the garden, and have been known to elbow small children out of the way so I get my turn on the giant tree swings.

But then there's the other half. The formal garden that nestles next to the house and gives off a definite sense that you can look but not touch. Unless maybe you play cards well – it was exchanged for gambling debts in 1618. In the late 17th

Century it was unused for a while, allowing the infamous Groombridge Gang of highway robbers to stalk the roads outside. Since then it has been privately owned, although the garden is now run as a commercial enterprise.

One thing I've noticed during my years of visiting gardens is that there's a definite difference between the gardens owned by one person and those owned by a trust, or even *the* National Trust. I find that with the former category it's much easier to walk round the gardens imagining they are my own. What would I change? What would I love the most? Where would I sit and drink my morning coffee?

Here, at Groombridge, I know I'd rush out every morning to walk round the knot garden that is laid out as tightly as it might have been in the

A bench in the formal garden

17th Century before the fashion for landscape gardening swept so many of our formal gardens away. I could even hear the swish of petticoats rounding the narrow corners and realised, for the first time, that this would have caused the box to bruise and so scent the air as you walked. I resisted the urge to play with the giant chess set and walked instead along the Apostle walk, trying to remember my Convent school education so I could name each of the twelve yews. I couldn't tell which was Judas though.

It was summer when I went so I was hoping for a sensory sniff in the white rose garden, which contains twenty varieties of white rose in celebration of the 200-year ownership by the Waller family, but it was more about the eyes than the nose for me this time. Also an eyeful are the peacocks, who seemed to spend a lot of time 'on parade' – even appropriately in the Peacock walk.

As you might expect from a formal garden, this is very organised. White roses, blue and yellow plants in the Drunken garden where Conan Doyle (who came from nearby Crowborough and so would probably have visited often) set his Sherlock Holmes story, *The Valley of Fear,* and in the Oriental garden, delicate Japanese maples trembling like shy ballerinas about to audition.

A central thread of the film *The Draughtsman's Contract* is the battle against nature. In the 17th Century, gardens were the deliberate result of architectural manipulation aimed at making the outside 'safe'. They were a reminder not only of life, but of death too. Now of course we don't have the Groombridge Gang waiting at the end of the drive, nor are we likely to lose our fortunes over one game of cards, and if anything the land around the garden gates is as manicured as that inside, but it's still good to go to a garden that reminds you that gardens aren't passive – the best ones will take you on a roller-coaster of the senses as heady as any theme park.

A peacock strutting his stuff at Groombridge Gardens

31

The Landscape of Love

She imagines sex with him
to be like this knot garden:

nature trimmed and framed
into a triumph of geometry

until she's espaliered,
clinging to the wall

of him, as apostle straight
he checkmates her,

enters a secret door
at the moat's edge

searching for shade
under the drum yews,

but even as she unties herself
the knots keep hold, re-form

and he's peacock-strutting again
over clematis clinging borders,

falling into the drunken garden
because she doesn't have a clue

how they tipped so fast
into abandonment.

Skin reveals itself in squares
on a body so tightly laced

it's a rose-scented death,
white after white after white.

A visitor who stayed too long at Groombridge Place?

Simple sign to the Labyrinth at All Saints Church

8   The Labyrinth at All Saints Church, Tudeley

In the churchyard at Tudeley there is a turf labyrinth open for anyone who wants to walk it. Historically, labyrinths were a feature of many medieval cathedrals and it was thought that those who couldn't make a pilgrimage to the Holy Land walked the labyrinth instead. Poignantly, given the current conflict in Syria, the model for this one found in a peaceful English graveyard has been taken from a design found in Damascus.

Unlike a maze, you can't get lost in a labyrinth. Instead you follow its single winding path to the centre. The frequent turns and shifts make it a powerful experience, not least because just as you feel you have reached the centre you are taken back to the outside. So perhaps it's not surprising that when you reach the heart, you pause. It isn't easy to leave. At Tudeley, there is a simple wood carving of two clasped hands in the middle as a symbolic representation of being held in safety.

I was lucky to have the perfect companion to walk the labyrinth with me in poet and poetry therapist, Victoria Field (and her dog, Poppy). Perfect also because it was her first visit to the church, so I could experience – through her – the wonder of entering such a simple building as this country church in a quiet village…

… and being taken by surprise by the beauty and magnificence of the stained glass windows designed by Marc Chagall inside.

Every time I visit I see something different, and I wonder if it is because of whom I visit the church with. During a trip several years ago a very patient friend taught me to stand close enough and long enough to see the artist's scratchings on the windows, which now make the design come alive.

This time, I couldn't help but notice how the light from the windows seems to spill over on to every other surface around. It is almost as if Chagall wanted to colour the world. There is a mixture of personal and public tension with this gift of the commission of a world famous master to remember the death of one twenty-one-year old local girl, Sarah d'Avigdor-Goldsmid, who died by drowning in 1963. The original plan was to have just one window, but when Chagall agreed, after some persuasion, to take on the commission, he visited Tudeley and, after seeing the church, was reputed to have said, 'It's magnificent, I will do them all.' It took over 15 years for all eleven windows to be completed, and their beauty is breathtaking.

So when we walked the labyrinth again, our hearts and minds were still full of the windows, and the slight breeze, birdsong and rustle of leaves added to the experience of taking time out. We seemed even more aware of the differences of light and shade. Even our glasses for a 'breakfast picnic' by the labyrinth – although plastic and definitely not beautiful – insisted on making their own reflections on the grass.

One of Marc Chagall's windows inside the church at Tudeley

Spilling Over

And after two churches,
a picnic breakfast
amongst the graves,
a missed turn
down country lanes,
there's still too much to say.

Our words are stained glass
overspilling windows,
the extra circle
round the labyrinth,
a second language
stitched in satin.

I follow you to your car,
waving as you drive away,
and like an ancient echo
from a cracked yew,
continue our conversation
all my way home.

*The knot garden,
Marle Place*

9 Marle Place Gardens and Gallery, Tonbridge

When I told a friend I was going to Marle Place, she told me she loved 'the art garden'. And when I got there, after driving under arching tunnels of trees my mum always called 'cathedrals', a woman rushed up to tell me I was getting the garden to myself. She'd been walking round, she said, and she'd been the only person. 'We are so lucky,' she repeated.

In fact, there were several other visitors, but the garden is designed in a series of rooms so it was possible to imagine that I was alone. I certainly didn't feel shepherded through from one bit to another as I have done in other gardens. Which is fortunate because this is a garden to amble slowly around and enjoy a feast for the senses, and not just in the scented garden.

The Victorian Gazebo, Marle Place

It is rare now to be able to visit a garden with no road noise. Just birds, trees rustling, and when you find them, the chickens.

And the art? Well, if you go in the Autumn you may catch the annual Sculpture Show where I have to admit the art added to and enhanced the beauty of the plants around it rather than shouting so loudly it dominated everything else. Some were witty, others more organic, and I was surprised at how it encouraged me to start noticing the sculptural quality of both the plants and the garden itself.

But because the house and gardens have been the family home of the Williams family for the last forty years, and definitely feel a personal creation, I was left with a feeling more domestic than 'arty'. An example was the freshly-picked apples from the garden sold individually in the shop to raise money for the local hospice, which summed up how this garden has its priorities right.

A view through the hedge

The News from the Kitchen Garden

is earthshattering,
a blackbird's made its nest
in the hawthorn tree,
and breaking as I write,
seedlings planted a month ago
are bursting forth, teasing

us with rainbow hints,
but if you rub a leaf
between finger and thumb
you can smell summer
already; a baby kicks its legs
in response at the clouds

Marle Place's productive vegetable garden

rolling over like news tape,
while over by the swings,
a camellia leads an uprising
of blood red against the privet,
tulips and bluebells form a coalition,
and even the grass strengthens its position

near where this morning, at five past eleven,
dizzy with dandelion flowers
the cat let a pigeon fly free,
while propped up against the wall
already warming itself for glory,
the first rosebud waits for her cue.

The topiary bear at Penshurst – symbol of the Sidney family

10   Penshurst Place and Gardens, Penshurst

Come to the Window

The pond's a perfect circle from above as if to show
how nothing need be set in stone, and even pain
can move and change – some days everything you know
turns out to be a lie and perspective's a trick to obtain
your trust, but isn't it better than a tale of woe
to smile and laugh in a garden set out to entertain —
topiary beasts, flower flags, beauty allowed to flow
so naturally you engage heart first then brain.
Maybe it's a waste that the peony border won't stay
fresh for long but come winter the wind will blow
into your dreams until you can remember the way
those bawdy flowers blush as if caught in the throes
of a delicious secret truth. There's no corner for spite
to hide in circles, and that's how I want to write.

I always think of Penshurst Place as a true writers' garden. This isn't just because it was the home of one of the great 16th Century English poets, Sir Philip Sidney, or the muse for Ben Johnson's poem, 'To Penshurst'.

Perhaps it is because it is still attracting writers today. There are regular literary events at both the house and garden; dramatist and short story writer, Gaye Jee, can be found guiding sometimes, and where else would you receive a reply to your email in verse from the office?

But this isn't the only reason to love Penshurst. It has a very special feel which comes from the fact that it is still the family home of the De L'Isles. An exhibition of family portraits and photographs over generations gives a glimpse of the private side of the house and garden and it's surprisingly poignant to see a picture of a small boy playing in one corner of the garden, followed by his graduation photograph from university, and then walking the grounds as a future owner. It must be a very different experience to live somewhere where every corner reminds you that you are just looking after this place for a future generation, just as those from the past have cared for it for you.

Because it's close to my home, I see this eleven-acre garden at many different times of the year, and it's hard to say which is the most beautiful. Even the winter months, when the hedges come into their own and the borders are ghosts of the colour that will come in spring, are special. I have spent frozen afternoons writing in fingerless gloves on one of the stone benches, and transporting myself back to the 16th Century when the garden was first laid out almost as it is today. It's impossible not to wonder if Sir Philip Sidney sat there writing too.

A Sidney family helmet (with porcupine)

The garden is heavy with views –from inside the garden or within the garden down hedge-lined paths, and also from the parkland outside where the garden is framed as if for a picture. There's an outdoor theatre where my children used to 'perform'; the white garden; a Jubilee 'carpet' with bedding laid out as a Union Jack, and an eighty-foot double herbaceous border which looks as if it has been painted by designer George Carter with hot red colours at the front leading to cooler blues at the back.

Our family favourites though are the topiary bear and porcupine that guard the garden. The porcupine is the symbolic animal of the Sidney family, and may seem a strange choice, but in ancient times it was believed that porcupines could throw their quills at an enemy. (Did you know that a group of porcupines is called a 'prickle'?)

Definitely not prickly is one of the other attractions of the garden at Penshurst Place, the hundred yard Peony Border. If you are lucky enough to visit at its prime (in June), I swear the memory of the sweet scent, which somehow smells of the colour pink, will keep you swooning all year. It's perhaps a glimpse of what it must be like to be a sheepdog, proud owners of 200 million olfactory cells in comparison to our measly five million. I'm still thinking of it now as the December rain lashes down outside. Due to demand, the office at Penshurst operates an email list, allowing you to sign up to be informed when the peonies are at their finest. I love how, in a time when we get most things we want with a touch of a button, we still wait patiently for flowers.

I was grateful to Gaye for pointing out something I had not noticed before, and that is how much of the garden plays with perspective. It was the pond with its Hercules statue at the front of the house that grabbed my attention. It looks like an oval from the ground while making a perfect circle when seen from the first floor reception room.

And so I took all of these things, and one of Sir Philip Sidney's sonnets as my writing inspiration. Sometimes the poems come easily, with a theme – personal or general – driving the words; sometimes it's the emotion of the garden I hope to represent; and with others, I'm trying to tell a story. In this case, it was form. Sidney was famous for his sonnets,

The view of the pond from the first-floor window at Penshurst Place

and I'd written pages in my journal before I realised that by using Sidney's line-ends in his poem 'Astrophel and Stella', I could mirror how it felt to be so safely enclosed by all the different borders in the garden.

The front drive
to Knole House

11 Knole Park, Sevenoaks

Of course, if we were being pedantic it shouldn't be Sevenoaks any more because it's been Oneoaks ever since the 1987 Great British Hurricane brought six of the town's mighty trees down.

Knole still sits in the middle of the town, though, not caring how many trees remain. After all, the park has been a deer park since medieval times and thanks to the National Trust is now open to walkers. Perhaps it's not surprising that passing time means so little to a house that is built around time, with its 365 rooms, 52 staircases, 12 entrances and 7 courtyards. The house has a grand façade, and it always gives me a thrill to drive right up to it before parking on the grass, as if one of its famous owners, Vita Sackville-West, is going to swing open the front door of the house and invite me to tea. There are formal gardens at the back, but for me it's always been the deer park that is the main attraction.

The expanse of the park encourages you to stride out, rather as Vita Sackville-West must have done in her breeches and boots. There's a lovely extract in a letter written by Virginia Woolf about Vita, 'Why she writes is a puzzle to me. If I were she, I should merely stride with 11 elk hounds behind me, through my ancestral woods.'

Kasia at Knole

I wasn't surprised recently to read that being able to focus on natural distant horizons supports wellbeing because, after a day spent walking in Knole Park and only managing to cover a small fraction of its 1,000 acres, I wondered why we kid ourselves we can cope without regular nourishment from the countryside. There are certain landscapes that dig themselves deep into our bones, almost as if we are the plants they are cultivating. We need them to survive. Knole is one of these for me. Best is when the gorse is out and there's a heady scent of honey. It reminds me of one of my grandmother's sayings, 'When the gorse ceases flowering, kissing goes out of the window.'

Actually best of all is to go with a small child. Not only do they see things you might miss, but they know exactly where the best rainbows are to jump in.

But what was more surprising was that even amongst such openness, there's also a feeling of being shut out. Like most visitors, my Sunday walks here are only a temporary possession. The gates are shut tight at closing time.

Perhaps I just think this way because of the fascination I've had with Vita Sackville-West's story since I was a child. Although she was the only child, because of the family's insistence on primogeniture, Knole went instead to her uncle, Charles. Apparently she never quite got over the loss, even after she created probably the most famous garden in England at Sissinghurst with her husband, the diplomat Harold Nicholson.

Then, I came across a story about how Vita had been given a small key to the grounds. She only used it very rarely but kept it with her at all times. And on one walk, where we came across a white stag, I had a vivid image of Vita walking in moonlight through the grounds that would never be truly hers.

A white stag at Knole

How to Leave Paradise

Stiff-backed, stiff-legged, each step working against gravity, head turned forward, chin lifted.

Without a backwards glance, knowing to do so would let down the house and all it stands for.

To feel in your pocket the weight of a key, a small lead key barely bigger than your own thumbnail.

In hotel rooms, from Monte Carlo to Teheran, to secrete the key under your pillow, to wake with the brand of home on your cheek.

And you build your own paradise, plant by plant, your fingers plunging deep into the soil, caressing the roots, a goddess of the earth.

For your most prized design to be a ghost garden, a white shadow of all you miss.

To leave the earth sometimes for a tower, the work of hands for the mind, to escape into dreams of a woman becoming a man, to stride through those gates again, to have no need of a key, nestling even now in your pocket, the weight of it keeping you grounded.

One night, you look up at the moon and think that just a few miles away the same moon is looking down on a doe you hadn't seen born, although you used to know them all.

And surely what happens at moonlight isn't real, so you can't be judged. The time of luna-tics, werewolves, transformations. You take your wolfhound, grandson of the one you bur-ied there, doesn't a dog deserve to know the bones of its family too, use your key to walk along the moonlight path, and for your feet to recognise home again, the heft of it.

To take that once-used key with you to your grave. And, in the English way, never to speak of it again.

*Peace at
Ightham Mote*

12   Ightham Mote, Sevenoaks

Shhh… this is a garden that's just waking up. When I visited it just after it had re-opened after a winter break, it reminded me of when I was a kid and it snowed overnight so I'd run outside as soon as I could – in pyjamas – to be the first to make footsteps on this new white land.

And every time I've visited this garden, I discover it all over again. Maybe because it's situated in a valley so you drive down to it, and then there's the moat that surrounds the timber framed house, which gives it an air of Sleeping Beauty's castle.

Over the last decade, its owners, the National Trust, have done a good job in kissing the fourteen-acre garden back to life, and are now restoring some of the 19th-Century planting. This has included the North Lake, the ornamental pond and the 18th-Century cascade in the woodland garden. Currently on the list is the South Lake, and soon the garden's water features will be fully restored back to their original marvelousness.

Garden restoration is never straightforward. There's an argument between those who believe a garden will always be changing, so it provides a false record to maintain it as it might have been at any set period of time, and those who believe that freezing the garden this way gives a true sense of the larger historical context. Now with archaeology, plant records and contemporary accounts, we can find out just what a garden would have been like. But what's missing, in my view, is the help to imagine what we – as the garden visitors – would have been like in the 16th, 17th and 18th Centuries. How exciting it must have been to see a cascade in full flow for the first time. Or to gain access to the private part of the house, such as the 15th-Century courtyard at Ightham Mote. Just imagine what it would have been like to see a particular plant specimen for the first time from a country you will never get to visit, and may not have even heard of before.

Perhaps in the 19th Century, you might have seen your first Great Dane dog at Ightham Mote. Would you have thought it a horse? Certainly Dido must have been a pampered pooch because the kennel, which still exists in the courtyard, is the only Grade 1 listed dog house in the country!

The house and garden are sunk in the countryside, keeping it enclosed from the rolling hills around, but this had the advantage that when I left Ightham Mote to take advantage of the walks around, I felt on top of the world. In fact, I ended up walking to Knole and back on the nicely signposted circular walk, and seeing both houses from a different angle, as you always do on foot.

A view on the walk from Ightham Mote to Knole Park

Walking the Dog

Today he is in charge, lead
looped at his side as he walks

the dog, smiling and keeping
in step as they bound over

the horizon. Only he knows
how yesterday the dog took over,

how he didn't dare open his eyes
in case it was sitting there,

teeth bared, paws on his shoulders,
the bulk of it blocking out the sun;

they stayed like that, prey and preyed,
and it didn't matter how many times

he told the child inside not to be afraid,
that the dog just wanted to be friends.

*The General Wolfe public
house in Westerham*

13   Quebec House, Westerham

The General's Mother Sends Him a Recipe for Consumption

Take a peck of garden snails
You were fourteen, a man several years,

wash them in beer, put them in an oven
full of stories from your father,
the house too small that day

and let them stay till they are done crying
you came running I didn't need to read
the commission in your hand,

then with a knife and cloth
instead got to work packing,
had to trust I'd taught you enough

pitch ye green from them
kindness, compassion, to put others first.

and beat ye snails all in a stone mortar
All your army reports glowed,
your progression almost too fast.

then take a quart of green earthworms
We thought a wife would settle you, chose a fine girl but

slice them through ye middle
your father said at least you knew your own mind

and stew them with salt
so I wept in secret, at least I did that,

then wash them and beat them
smiled when my choice married your best friend,

ye pott being first put into ye still
even played with the babies as they grew up.

with two hand fulls of angelica, a quart of rosemary flowers
I slept with your letters under my pillow,

then ye snails and worms, the egrimony, red clover
wrote out my receipts lovingly for you,

then pour in three gallons of milk
tried not to let a mother's worry speak too loudly,

keep your still covered all night
though I feared what might happen if you lost your softness,

this done, stir it not
knowing that a broken heart rarely heals straight

distill it with moderate fire
so we held our heads high,
even when the news was rotten.

ye patient must take two spoonfulls at a time
Now I pick flowers, never let myself forget.

To be honest, I wanted to see the small vegetable garden (actually just a strip) at Quebec House more than I wanted to find out about General James Wolfe, the so-called 'Conqueror of Quebec'. Quebec House, then known as Spiers House, was Wolfe's childhood home, and the garden has been planted by the National Trust with the flowers and vegetables that would have grown in the 1730s.

I'd got hold of a booklet of Mrs Wolfe's household recipes already, and matched as many species of plants in the garden to the recipes to get a real feeling of Georgian housekeeping. There are three niches in the wall to hold bee 'skeps', hives made from woven straw, ideal to pollinate the quinces and

The vegetable garden at Quebec House

grapevine that still grow there. Some of the recipes, though, call for more exotic ingredients – the oranges, lemons and carp would have come from neighbouring Squerry's Court where George Warde, childhood friend and playmate of James Wolfe, lived. It's easy to imagine the young James coming back with an orange from the Court's exotic orangery as a gift, perhaps in exchange for one of his mother's recipes such as the one below:

For the Collick: Of the best Rhubarb 2 oz, Virginia Snakeweed ½ oz. Infuse em in a quart of Brandy. Take at night when ye go to bed. Mrs Wolfe.

What I hadn't expected was a strange dissonance between the marigolds, leeks and espaliered apple trees of the vegetable garden and the exhibition about General Wolfe's military career in the stables just on the other side of the garden wall.

The large oil painting of his death at the Battle of Quebec, by Benjamin West, forms the centre of the exhibition, and shows him as a beautiful, red-coated hero under a British flag and surrounded by his men on the battlefield. The rest of the exhibition focuses on his military life, culminating in the Siege of Quebec which Wolfe 'won' for Britain over the French. The victory came at the cost not just of Wolfe's life but of the lives of many innocent people. He was openly ruthless, vowing in a letter to his commander in chief, Jeffrey Amhurst, to leave 'a trail of famine and destruction behind.'

This was fascinating – on one side of the wall, evidence of a mother who took so much care growing good food for her family and on the

A bee skep, traditionally woven straw hive

other, a son who had used hunger as a weapon, even as he was writing home for his mother's recipes to help him look after his troops. General Wolfe had received his much-longed for military orders when he was still effectively a child (fourteen years old) and later, rejected his mother's first choice of a woman who could be his wife, suffering heartbreak when his own choice then rejected him.

In fact the story of this so-called public man mirrored the private anguishes that still go on in any family with a headstrong child. I went back for another look at the vegetable garden – this time imagining a mother who sees quite a different man than the public would have seen, and who grew plants and vegetables here for her family, scribbling down recipes of what her family liked.

The poem I eventually wrote mixed my thoughts with one of Mrs Wolfe's recipes. Because even heroes need someone to worry about whether they are 'growing straight', and sometimes heartache can be soothed through hard gardening.

*Emma Darwin's flower borders at Down House,
as she might have designed them*

14 Down House, Downe

The twisting country roads to Charles Darwin's family house are a lesson in survival in themselves. But once you're there, the house and gardens are a sanctuary. As, indeed, they must have felt to the Darwin family when controversy over Darwin's work was at its highest.

The new curator, English Heritage, has recreated Down House very much as a family home, complete with a branch propped up against the house as if the Darwin children are just about to climb out of their nursery window and into the garden, exactly as they once did.

English Heritage has also managed to show how the garden was a living laboratory for Darwin's experiments. A sign on the lawn explains that it was not just a place for Darwin to relax in, but where he recorded myriad plant species that grew there for a number of years, the 'lawn plot experiment' he described in *The Origin of Species*. In fact it's harder to think of this famous scientist relaxing on the garden bench than down on his knees counting plants. Next to the sign is a bamboo-fenced square to mark out the sample plot, just as he would have used in the experiment at the time; it looks curiously like one of my favourite paintings, Albrecht Dürer's 'Great Piece of Turf', where the weeds – plantain, meadow grass and dandelion flowers – are pictured with such reverence that they could be precious flowers.

At the edge of the garden is the meadow in which Darwin, with the help of the nanny, tried to sort out how many wild species of plants would have grown naturally. I wonder if the nanny would have applied for the job if she'd known she'd be following the children's father through a field for hours, taking notes and counting individual stalks of grass.

If you visit Down House, I suggest you take the garden tour. There is so much I would otherwise have missed, such as the 'worm hole', the record of an experiment Darwin carried out with his son. Until it was pointed out, it looked like a hole for a washing line. And then there is the greenhouse full of carnivorous plants, a type discovered and investigated by Darwin in 1860. I arrived at 'plant lunchtime'; one of the Venus Fly Traps was bloated with a fly caught in its green belly. This plant, called by Darwin 'the world's most wonderful flower', emits digestive fluids in which the insect is slowly dissolved until the proteins are absorbed in the leaf. The whole process takes about a week apparently, but I didn't hang around to see.

The fact that the garden was clearly used as a laboratory for Darwin made me feel for Emma who, as the gardener of the family, attempted beauty as well as science. The flower borders have now been recreated as they might have looked under her aesthetic eye, and after watching the Venus Fly Trap in action, they seemed even more full of colour, richness and scent.

But the bit of the tour that delighted me most was Darwin's circular 'thinking path'. When he was at home, he would walk five laps round the sandy path through the copse twice a day. To keep count, he would leave a pebble each time he passed the starting point but his children would sometimes creep out to either remove one, or add one, so he'd never be quite certain how many times he had gone round.

A patch on the front lawn recreates one of Darwin's experiments

Walking with Darwin

It was on the second round,
only three pebbles
left on the bend,
that I began to feel
lighter,
placing my feet
where he once paced,
until I could guess
when it's you about to overturn
the world, you would need
something like this,
the sound of laughter,
how even as your children
played, you kept
on the path you started,
the end and the beginning
in one sand circle;
what's one more round
when not even love
can disrupt the plan?

Red House, with its garden porch,
Pilgrim's Rest, on the right

15   Red House, Bexleyheath

Digging Up William Morris's Potatoes

It's a hot potato, mashed, smashed,
boiled to a turn, it's got its jacket on,
been chipped, French fried, finely
diced, topped and crowned, but

is it beautiful?

We arrange them in a china bowl,
pink earth eggs, dark scented
like honest women, skins
blooming with imperfections, but

is it useful?

As they struggle to breathe in the
kitchen air, tubers blindly groping
their way back to cold soil beds,
we heat water, watch as they fail to swim.

Peel it, roast it, serve it on the side,
Wedge it, spice it, nutmeg, salt and cream,
pocket warmer, peasant filler, fat
maker, famine causer, hot potato.

nearly turned back when I got to the suburban street marked as the address for
Red House. I've read that gardens are best approached on foot from a distance to
get the context, but it was hard to imagine William Morris, who once proclaimed

that we should have nothing in our houses that was not beautiful or useful, building his first house on such a busy street, with speed bumps and speed signs against the curving red brick wall.

But once in through the wooden gates, there's an immediately calmer atmosphere. A huge tree sits in an oval patch of grass with a white metal bench all the way round the trunk, and the house itself, designed by the architect Philip Webb, has a recessed front door that welcomes you in. In medieval times, Chaucer's pilgrims would have passed nearby on their way to Canterbury. This connects nicely with Morris's passion for medieval architecture and I loved that he christened the garden porch, which is found at the back of the house, the 'Pilgrim's Rest' in honour of Chaucer.

One of William Morris's designs on display in the house

The house and garden were designed together, and although not much of the original design of the garden remains, it's hard not to use it as a viewing platform for the architectural angles and details. In fact, as I walked round the garden, I couldn't find one spot where I didn't see the house.

I deliberately went in autumn because I wanted to see the orchard in fruit, as the site had originally been an orchard when Morris found it in 1858, and some of the trees – apple, cherry, oak, yew, hazel and holly – remain. In the rest of the garden, the flowers and plants were an inspiration for Morris's own designs, so as I walked round, I had half an eye on looking out for the shapes and structures that might have appealed to him. I noticed teasels, dragon's lanterns, honesty leaves and pods just bursting open with orange berries. No sunflowers, although these are featured in a woodcut on display in the house so I imagine they were once a feature in the garden.

Part of Webb's design specification was that the house should be 'clothed' in traditional climbers such as roses, white jasmine and honeysuckle. Two pears on a curved branch were trying to knock against a very thin metal window frame, and blood-red grapes on a variegated vine provided a contrast to the rusty coloured brick walls. At the back, a sturdy apple tree branch provided what looked like a step out from a window shaped like a Bishop's mitre.

Fruit trees knocking at a Red House window

As I sat on the lawn, I remembered what William Morris's daughter, May, had written about the time the poet Swinburne lay in the orchard, his long red hair spread out on the grass, as she and her sister Jenny sprinkled rose petals on his face.

And if the house was designed to be looked at from the garden, so the garden forms pictures from different windows of the house. From the dining room window, gardeners doing what must have been the last mow of the season and a round window on the top landing offered a little square of plain glass to look out from a surrounding circle of hand-painted flowers and fruits.

Just the week before I visited Red House, I set my students the task of writing about the view from a character's bedroom so they could understand him or her better. Framed in his bedroom window, William Morris would have woken up to a tree with outstretched, even branches and a path leading beyond the lawn outside. On a windy night, Morris would have lain in bed listening to the creak and whistle of this tree.

The house has been taken back by the National Trust and is dedicated to the time William Morris spent there, but it has escaped feeling too much like a museum. It was good – if surprising – to see potatoes and apples on sale in the vegetable patch. How could I resist taking some home? William Morris loved his food so I think he would have approved. In fact, his greed led to a spectacularly good practical joke by his friend, Edward Burne-Jones, who had the sides of Morris's waistcoat secretly sewn up to persuade him he was putting on weight.

Perhaps this was the cause of the famous apple fight in the Red House Drawing Room which apparently left Morris with a black eye.

GO FOR A WALK AND PHOTOGRAPH OR DRAW AS MANY <u>RED</u> THINGS AS YOU CAN FIND ...

Peaceful borders at
St John's Jerusalem

16   St John's Jerusalem, Sutton-at-Hone

Green Thoughts

Better to fight than to be corseted
into bedding displays, bruised
for a passing scent, deadheaded.

Is this why thorns protect tender buds,
an uprooted mandrake screams, and Eve
took her chance, leaving paradise before Adam

discovered pruning? But then you come here,
St John's Jerusalem, and everywhere you look
time is gentled, a butterfly stays long enough

to fold its wings, a drop of blood
kissed safe in lace nests, and that door
in a tree will take you to another world.

After just one afternoon spent in the garden at St John's Jerusalem, I could see why Sir Stephen Tallents and his wife loved their home so much that they left it to the British people via the National Trust. Sir Stephen Tallents was a civil servant, responsible for promoting British interests abroad in the post First World War period. Amongst his commissions was the 1936 documentary, Night Mail, which featured a poem by W.H. Auden and music by Benjamin Britten.

I wonder if he kept his own garden in his mind as a corner of an ideal Britain, because there's something about its gentle rhythm that settles any discordance caused by the outside world's busyness. Perhaps it is because the garden remains surrounded by the square 13th-Century moat, fed by the River Darent, that the Knights of the Order of St John of Jerusalem would have fished in. It is certainly easy to think of them sitting where the weeping willows dip their branches into the moat as if drinking, next to the Cedar of Lebanon and the thick trunked oaks with what look like little curved doors you could open into another world.

A butterfly alights on a plant at St John's Jerusalem

The Order of St John of Jerusalem owned this property from 1199. Originally formed to care for sick pilgrims, they evolved into providing armed escorts on pilgrimages and then became one of the most powerful political organisations in the late Middle Ages. The chapel of the Knights Hospitallers, also from the 13th Century, is still open, and is in fact where you buy tickets for the garden. The Order itself, after decades of violent battles and defeats, was revived with its original remit of caring for the sick, and eventually became the St John's Ambulance Association.

The St John's Jerusalem gardener, Will Gould, told me how there's a small red bloom to be found in every head of Queen Anne's Lace, found in abundance in the more formal flower garden. Apparently it represents a drop of blood from her finger when she was spinning. I had to look closely because, do you know, I have never noticed this before. And then, suddenly, everywhere I looked I saw new and beautiful things, a dropped petal that had been caught in the gossamer of a spider's web so it looked as if was forever suspended, the lacework in a butterfly's wings. The butterfly had landed gently on a cornflower as I watched, staying long enough for me to see how it stretched out its front feet, where its taste organs are, so it could feast on summer nectar.

I had arrived stressed at this garden, someone had cut me up on the motorway, another driver had hooted as I drove slowly to locate the garden's entrance. I had a deadline looming, and it seemed an indulgence to be visiting a garden. In fact, my senses were so stretched and acute that even the tree leaves rustling in the breeze seemed as if they were snapping at me. I left smiling at everyone else on the road, and with a sudden new vision as to how I could complete my deadline. It was a reminder that sometimes all we need is to relearn how to look at a garden.

A magical tree at St John's Jerusalem

The tower
at Sissinghurst

17 Sissinghurst Castle, Cranbrook

For many garden lovers, Kent equals Sissinghurst, and this has become less a garden than a national institution. A garden to be ticked off in any tour of English gardens. A garden to be collected and name-dropped when talking about gardens. For all these reasons, I was almost tempted to leave it out of my tour, but then I visited again and fell in love for the hundredth time with the romanticism of the tower that dominates the garden, the generous planting, the profusion of flowers. Even brushing off magnolia petals to sit down on a stone bench seemed like a moment to capture in a poem.

The trouble, of course, is that I'm not the only one to feel this, and so a visit to the garden at Sissinghurst is to be part of the crowd. A polite, garden-loving crowd admittedly, but still apt to fight you to a bench with that particularly good view or the last scone in the tea room. Perhaps this is part of Sissinghurst's own history though. A plaque at the entrance to the tower is dedicated simply to 'V Sackville-West who made this garden', and when it first opened to the public one weekend in June 1938 for Mrs Elsie Wragg's Yellow Book, the forerunner to the National Gardens Scheme, it was Vita who took the money. She used to call the visitors 'the shillings' in honour of the shilling they paid to raise money for the Queen's Nursing Institute.

Vita was in charge of the planting, and her husband, Harold Nicholson, was responsible for the design. Looking at pictures, the 'shillings' would have seen a similar garden to the one we walk around now. The lines in the newly mown lawn and clipped hedges contrasting with borders bursting with clusters of grape hyacinths, the intricately patterned lanterns of snake's head fritillary bulbs and shy pale hellebores in what Vita called 'profusion, even extravagance and exuberance, within confines of the utmost linear severity'.

In 2013, the National Trust appointed a new head gardener, Troy Scott Smith, the first male head gardener in the garden's history. After Vita, there had been a series of women gardeners: Pam Schwerdt and Sibylle Kreutzberger, then Sarah Cook and Alexis Datta. I wonder if we will see a change in style as a result. Do men garden differently from women? The cliché might be to think of a male garden as one of straight lines and logical organisation so it's reassuring to read that Mr Scott Smith is actually looking to loosen up some of the 'tidiness' that has crept in recently, perhaps taking it back to the self-taught Vita Sackville-West's days, when she could write:

My garden all is overblown with roses,
my spirit all is overblown with rhyme.

Given the coachloads of visitors Sissinghurst attracts, there can be a slight feeling that you are on a conveyor belt, but because the nine-acre garden is famously laid out in a series of rooms, it should still be possible to jump off the tracks. I found the answer to be to look at the detail rather than the whole. In the famous white garden, I was entranced all over again to see that although no plant is actually white, the pale green foliage and petals allow the impression of an almost translucent lightness. Texture became all, and it was hard not to reach out and touch the soft peachiness of the lambs ear leaves, or to push a thistle spike against my finger. And roses, roses everywhere.

Linear severity and joyous planting at Sissinghurst

When I went in late spring, the bulbs were carpeting the gardens and fruit trees were aching with buds. Pink camellias shocked against brick walls, and in the vegetable garden, sweet peas, nasturtiums and marigolds jostled for space.

This might seem like a mundane list of plants but that's part of the charm. For such a famous garden, Sissinghurst still has all the elements of a garden you and I might plant. It manages to keep the atmosphere of a much-loved experiment, such as the seat of chamomile that was being planted in one of the stone benches when I visited. This 'can do' attitude comes across strongly in the weekly gardening columns Vita Sackville-West wrote in the *Observer* for fifteen years. She would have composed them up in her writing room in the tower, with one of the two weathercocks creaking above her, and perhaps taking a break to look out over the entire nine acres of garden. So, as she advocated self-seeding and abundant planting to her readers, she must have had the perfect view of how her flowers competed with and softened her husband's 'linear severity'.

The orchard at Sissinghurst

Cicero said that if you have a garden and a library, you have everything you need. Well, Sissinghurst proves that to plant the best garden you also need a little bit of rebellion in your heart as well.

The Garden Visitor

And it happens so slowly
you have time to wonder
if there is a verb for it,
to gardeninify, to absorb
through feet and purse
and guidebook and heart,
the essence of a place
until you are the garden,
walking in dreams as fertile
as the wildflower path
you capture on camera,
the sounds of a stream
mirroring blood running
through your veins,
each jump and start
a wave of a season ticket.
Come winter, you'll be visiting
still, the curve of your back
echoing the tree on the hill
that the wind has moved
so often you could say
it has surrendered,
but even as you park your car
and pay your entrance fee,
you feel the garden through your skin,
your spirit buries itself in the soil
until you're not sure if you
have ever been 'just visiting'.

WALK IN A GARDEN AND WRITE PORTRAITS OF TWO PLANTS. IMAGINE THEM HAVING A CONVERSATION.

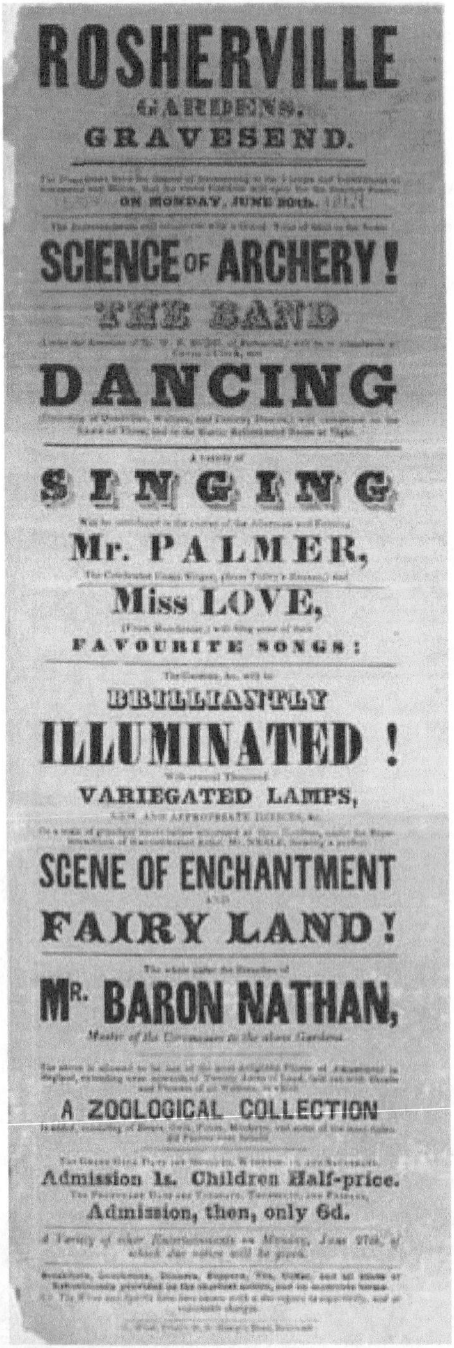

A poster advertising Rosherville Gardens

18   Rosherville Pleasure Gardens, Gravesend

There is a story about Sir Stanley Gervase-Gervase at Rosherville Gardens which is ghastly in its perfection of detail. It seems that Sir Stanley – but I can't tell you.
P.G. Wodehouse

Like a Disneyland for grown ups, a ball to which everyone is invited and where no one quite stops dancing – that's how I picture the pleasure gardens that were such a feature of the 1800s. They were described as places of 'divine playfulness', a perpetual holiday, and although Vauxhall Gardens in South London was the most famous, in the 1840s and 1850s, hundreds of visitors travelled down to Kent by steamboat from London to visit the Rosherville Pleasure Gardens.

When they were created in one of the disused chalk pits in Northfleet in 1837, they were called the 'Kent Zoological and Botanical Gardens Institute' and had the lofty cultural aim of being a place for the best society to enjoy the zoological gardens and fine planting. However, by the mid-1800s, the emphasis was fully on pleasure rather than garden. Here's how local boy, Charles Dickens, Jr, described Rosherville in his 1881 *Dickens's Dictionary of the Thames*:

Besides the tea and shrimps so dear to the heart of the Gravesend excursionist, other refreshments of a more substantial and stimulating character can be obtained at very reasonable rates... There is a conservatory about 200 feet long, a bijou theatre, a maze, museum, 'baronial hall,' occasionally used for dancing, but more often for purposes of refreshment. There is a very good fernery and a bear-pit, and some two miles of walks are held out as additional inducements to the excursion public ... it is quite feasible to pass that 'Happy Day' which in the advertisements is always coupled with the name of Rosherville.

Hmmm... it seems that part of the guarantee of a 'Happy Day' came from an unofficial rule of secrecy, or 'what happens in Rosherville stays in Rosherville'. As one contemporary account from 1892 notes, 'The maze wasn't bad fun. Four of us lost ourselves there; two were of the other sex.' And all for an admission charge of only sixpence.

I couldn't actually find evidence of any plants that were grown at Rosherville after the Garden's famous Master of Ceremonies, ex-dancing teacher Mr Baron Nathan, took control in 1842. Instead attractions including a human cannonball and a father and son team of tightrope walkers took over, and excavations at Northfleet in 2012 uncovered the original bear pit. I have a party trick that involves eating a crème caramel from a plate using no hands, but Mr Baron Nathan trumps that. He trumps everyone. As the evening's entertainment reached fever pitch, he would come out, blindfolded, to dance a hornpipe on a stage on which thirty-two fresh eggs had been placed – without breaking one.

I managed to buy an old postcard of the gardens online. The picture is a standard black and white photograph of the now disappeared bandstand, but the pencil message on the back was a bit of luck given the picture I had formed of Rosherville: *E, see you Thursday at 11 by the wall. Come alone. William.*

A Letter to Mr Baron Nathan from a Lady in the Audience

I'm not normally keen on gardens
but was drawn by the posters,
Be prepared for anything,
so when I saw you, blindfolded
and dancing – hello, I thought;
the way that velvet suit encased
a body so smoothly oval
I wanted to tap you here,
and there, to take my spoon to you,
consume slowly down to your yolk –
we'd wobble for sure by breakfast –
but then young Master Gellini (ten
years old) announced his terrific flight
direct from the cliffs for our pleasure
and delight. Steamboats raced,
rockets showered and though
I'd yet to see a flower,
you took again
to the stage, hornpiping
with that stylish flip of calf
over a carpet of thirty other eggs.
Oh yes, we'll unshell each other
under fairy land illuminations,
a pyrotechnical finale for a fall
more brilliant than in that other Eden;
at Rosherville where paradise
grows wild as a weed in every bed.

One of Roderick Cameron's man-made
ruins, Great Comp Garden

19   Great Comp Garden, Near Sevenoaks

Great Comp garden, near Sevenoaks in Kent, is a remarkably personal and quirky garden, wrapped round an elegant 17th-Century house. Dotted around the seven-acre lands are a number of 'ruins' which, by the time you spot the second one, you realise must have been created as ruins and be the work of the same person. They offer an interesting tension between wild imagination and order, classical romance and technical challenge, drama and horticultural excellence.

So perhaps it wasn't surprising that as I was walking around, I was thinking about who had planted this garden (and the ruins). There's such a sense of originality here that it comes bursting through from the past and into the present.

The clue came in the book I bought on impulse at the ticket office, *The Life of an Amateur* by Roderick Cameron. The writing was a mix of pomposity and humour, so energetic that it felt as if someone was speaking it into my ear as I read. As I sat on a bench to finish it, I could imagine Mr Cameron's Scottish accent echoing round the garden. Particularly his question, 'Why if I and Great Comp are so great are we not famous?' Which I must admit I was asking myself. This is indeed one of Kent's hidden treasures.

Roderick and his wife, Joy, moved to Great Comp in 1957 and created the garden we see today, ruins and all. He was inspired by his time in the Royal Engineers during the Second World War where he'd visited Italian cities, particularly the ancient Roman ruins. His creations at Great Comp are all built with stones taken from the garden.

For nearly twenty years, Roderick and Joy Cameron carried out all the planning, planting and running of the garden themselves. As well as the ruins, there is a fine collection of salvias, over seventy magnolia trees, large areas of informal planting, an Italian garden with a collection of Mediterranean plants. There is a wilderness at the back with winding paths through the willows, oaks and specimen trees tricking the eye into thinking this is a much larger garden than it seems.

The garden is now run by the Great Comp Trust, and curator William Dyson. Although Roderick Cameron died in 2009, I imagine that the skeleton structure he designed is what gives the garden its cohesion. As he once said, even after the running had been taken over by the Trust: 'it is still my garden'.

I imagine it is the Trust we have to thank, not just for the sensitive and alive maintenance of the garden itself, but for possibly the most welcoming tea room ever in the old dairy with chairs and sofas draped with those rugs made from crocheted squares, and fairy lights everywhere. Perhaps best of all, there are shelves full of books to take and read by the wood burning stove.

In a small exhibition of photographs and cuttings about the garden, there's a photograph from the 1940s of six women entitled, 'Important ladies from the WI'. They are wearing loosely draped summer dresses and all six sport dashing hats. It made me think that hats for garden visiting should definitely make a come back, although I did like the group of elderly people walking round when I was there – they must have been in their seventies at least, and two of them were wearing jackets bearing the logo of an athletics team. I do hope they were active hurdlers and sprinters.

A view of the house from the garden

The Life of an Amateur

A collage of Roderick Cameron's words

It is not necessary to be a genius
to be a garden designer.
It will have been noticed
that my early life was devoid
of any interest in gardening.
The first ruin was the start,
the same ruins
could not have been built
by other people.
Although never much of a personality,
I spent one night
in the unfinished buildings
of Mussolini's 1942 Exhibition.
During the night, a plane
circled several times
and dropped a bomb,
led me to become
an expert on concrete.

I have made at least three
daily perambulations,
and noted for this diary,
our 70 magnolias coming,
gingkoes, field maples,
many common oaks to replace beeches.
The Liriodendron and *Magnolia veitchii*
stunning
and plenty of others, *Acer griseum,*
Malus tschonoskii, Parrotia,

Euonymus alatus, Cornus controversa
variegate.
We inspiring
need not be gigantic
or complex,
to many no doubt as dull
as ditchwater,
and such a contrast to my life
during my time on earth
never letting anyone complete
a sentence in committee or elsewhere,
at Great Comp I told them
just to do what I wanted.

I accept an element of truth in it all,
it is given to few to be
both popular and achieve something.
My late wife and I are not
of that company.
One of the last things
she said on her death bed was
'You never let me get a word in edgewise.'

If I were to presume to pass on advice,
be thankful for the sun,
let others worry about what follows.
No damage is a suitable note
to end my diary
on a note of optimism.

A bench at
Chartwell

20   Chartwell, Westerham

A Joyride Round the Garden

Venetian red leaving earth behind
before we can strap terre verte on.

Ambling round the rose
garden through to the white chair,
Jock by his side at the lake.

Scarlet lake ultramarine violet let
let cadmium lemon take us faster.

Black dog on his shoulder again,
and yet here, brick after brick calming
order, pattern of pleasing richness.

Unsettle with unknowing we only
think we see lamp black black light.

Back to earth, a child's house,
two trees for two daughters, an oblong
canvas waiting for history's brush.

And burnt sienna heats heats until purple
madder madder madder flake white.

The Prime Minister will decide himself
when he is most grateful. Thank you
for visiting. A day spent away is wasted.

visited Chartwell in spring, albeit on possibly one of the coldest days of the year, and as atmospherically misty and drizzly as any in winter. But Winston Churchill, who lived here from 1924 until his death at the age of 90 in 1965, famously said 'A day away from Chartwell is a day wasted', so I think he probably enjoyed all the seasons equally.

Evidence of Winston Churchill's famous wall-building

Besides, it doesn't feel to me that this is a particularly horticulturally sensitive garden, beautiful but most interesting for being Winston Churchill's private retreat. Certainly the man himself is still present everywhere you look. A nicely rusticated and worn bench resting against the house has his name in large capitals along the back, a contrast to the symmetrically placed and uniform benches elsewhere, which suggested to me that this was the bench he actually sat on. I hope so.

Walking round the garden, I could appreciate the sense of order, if not control, that must have been part and parcel of the life of such a successful politician. This was demonstrated in the walls crisscrossing the property. Famously, Winston Churchill built many of these himself as a way to relax. In fact, he became so adept at bricklaying that he joined the Guild of Bricklayers. I could see the attraction. It made me want to rush home and build my own wall. Imagine building something you can see growing with every brick AND being able to get it so exact. It appeals to all that is Virgo in me.

And as I stood on the mound outside the house looking down at the garden, I could also imagine him taking potshots at us visitors with our colourful umbrellas, or at the very least harrumphing in a corner somewhere at the 'invasion'.

Behind one of the low stone walls that run behind the house, you can find the graves of the Churchill family pets, including one for Jock, his favourite cat who kept him company for the last three years of his life. Jock would sit next to Winston Churchill's white garden chair as he fed the fish in the pond, and although I didn't see it, there is still a 'Jock' at Chartwell. Following Winston Churchill's request for a cat with four white paws and a white bib to always live at Chartwell, the National Trust have just introduced a lucky rescue cat, Jock VI, to his new home.

But a special part of the garden is the little playhouse that Winston Churchill built for his daughter, Mary, and called the Marycot. Apparently all visitors to the 'Big House' would come to the Marycot to eat dropscones made on the little oven there. As these visitors varied from Charlie Chaplin to Lawrence of Arabia, with some international statesmen thrown in for good measure, wouldn't you have loved to listen in to the conversations that must have taken place here?

In addition to the garden, Winston Churchill's art studio is worth a visit. He took up painting when he was forty, and finished more than 500 pictures over the next 48 years. His first exhibited painting was of winter sunshine at Chartwell and on display, next to his collection of carved wooden walking sticks, are several water-colours inspired by the colours in the garden. And in case you forget that Churchill didn't spend all of his time on 'hobbies', there is an exhibition of letters and memorabilia from his time in office. It made me laugh to read a letter to members of the civil service that went something like this: 'The Prime Minister wishes it to be recorded that the expression "most grateful" is not to appear in any letter for his signature. He says that he is the only person who can decide whether he is grateful or not.'

Fields of new rootstock at Brogdale

21 The National Fruit Collection, Brogdale

I wanted to include an orchard in this tour, not just because Kent is known for its apples but because of a certain apple tree in the garden of Eden. So where better than Brogdale, near Faversham, home of the National Fruit Collection?

I visited in October to see the harvest. There are pears, cherries, gooseberries, blackcurrants, and nuts growing here, but it was the apples I was particularly interested in. Over 2,300 varieties apparently, some with names that beg for a story to be written about them like Marriage Maker, and then there's Wealthy, and a descriptive if showy-offy Twenty Ounce. I wanted to taste them all.

The orchards are not just about being decorative or delicious though; the collection is run by Reading University for scientific purposes, and is one of the largest fruit collections in the world. Much of the work is centred around conserving genetic diversity and enabling crops to be adapted in the face of increasing pressures from pests and diseases, changing market requirements and the uncertainty of global climate change. You can see the new rootstock (smaller and more efficient) getting ready to take over apple production from their elders, rather like young army recruits lining up behind increasingly ancient Generals.

I bet the two 'Duchess of Oldenburg' trees, rare enough to be kept in their own separate row, look down on these upstarts. I could just imagine them gossiping together about how the rest of the apples in the field are letting the side down.

There's something about apples heavy on a tree that takes me straight back to childhood, when we just couldn't understand why it was forbidden to take an apple from a branch just because my mother claimed there were 'perfectly good windfalls' on the ground. Of course, as mini scrumpers, we would often help a particularly tasty-looking apple fall with a tug or two.

But luckily, Brogdale pick the apples for you and I finished my tour with a trip to the shop to buy a selection of apples from all the varieties on display. It was like healthy pick'n'mix, and a reminder of how much we have lost when we are offered just red or 'golden' apples at the supermarket.

Windfalls at Brogdale

A (nearly complete) alphabetical selection from the apple trees on sale at Brogdale: *Annie Elizabeth, Bloody Ploughman, Chorister Boy, Crawley Beauty, Doctor Hogg, Flower of the Town, George Carpenter, High View Pippin, Isaac Newton's Tree, Joybells, Katy, Lady Sudeley, Maidstone Favourite, Newton Wonder, Pitmaston Pine, Queen, Rosemary Russet, Sussex Mother, Tower of Glamis, Wadhurst Pippin.*

Night Fruit

A bobbing bouncing stream of apple skin snaking its way around the city, pips thrown mischievously through keyholes in the hope they'll take …

… the bite of apple flesh lodges in the Princess's throat until the prince moves her coffin to his house, the jolt of the carriage, and Gavin, who has become obsessional about apples, and who will, if you're not careful, tell you all day about the grafting and the harvesting of them, likes this story, even though his friends say it's a girl's story, but what he wants to know is what type of apple it was. Was it a Discovery, or an Egremont Russet, a Lord Lambourne, or a Merton Charm, until his mother says, it was a red apple, OK? And because she's exhausted, nearly out of patience, she kisses and leaves him. Gavin can't get to sleep. A red apple. Maybe a Bloody Ploughman, a King's Acre Pippin. Or a Red Windsor, considering that it was a Queen who gave the apple. He's still awake when his mother creeps in. It was a Pine Golden Pippin apple, she says, kissing him again although he's already had his night kiss. A russet, his mother whispers. Sweet.

… and the maggot hole you nearly miss, leading down to the core, the story hidden deep inside…

… why a Golden Delicious is allowed to be called that when it's neither golden nor delicious, this is what James asks his wife. A Green OK would be a better name, he says, and although Susanne tries to grunt as if she cares, he knows she doesn't and that this shouldn't, but does, matter. But also that neither of them will say anything. They never do. Later in bed, he will dream of being Paris but instead of judging the nymphs, he's chasing them, throwing hard apples as if he means to hurt, until one nymph, bored and bruised, stops and lobs one back. He sees her face as he catches the ball which has turned into a baby, and shocked awake, he reaches for Susanne. You're delicious, he surprises them both by saying, as they drift back, smiling, to sleep.

... windfalls they call them, as if the wind had picked them up and dropped them without thinking...

... an apple never falls far from the tree, the doctor says. He wants to know more about Gavin's father because this might help them to determine the severity of the symptoms. She says she doesn't know; she's hardened herself by now to the look she'll get, but this time round there's not even sympathy in the doctor's gaze. He is matter of fact as he outlines Gavin's future. It'll be hard work, he says, but you'll cope. And because she knows this too, and this is the first doctor she wants to confess to about how Gavin is her harvest and how it feels to be the worm, she starts to speak. He was called James, she says so quietly the doctor almost doesn't hear. He was married, I don't think he even knew my name.

... while high above, from New Zealand, Australia, Spain, America, frozen in crates, a uniform army of perfect apples fly in.

A view of Leeds Castle through the grounds

22   Leeds Castle, Maidstone

This Castle – in Kent, not Yorkshire as some people apparently think – is justly proud of historian Lord Conway's comment that it is the 'loveliest castle in the whole world'. Its origin dates from 1119, and six queens – Eleanor of Castile, Margaret of France, Isabella of France, Anne of Bohemia, Joan of Navarre, Catherine de Valois – have called the garden their own, perhaps walking by, as Lord Conway also said: '... the waters on an autumnal evening when the bracken is golden and there is a faint blue mist among the trees ...'.

What he doesn't mention is the fish, although a sign by the lake lists the provisions provided by the Castle to Henry VIII when he visited in 1520 on the way to meet Francois I at the Cloth of Gold Tournament. Amongst the more usual sheep, eels and chickens, it mentions three porpoises and one dolphin. Surely these wouldn't have survived here, would they? It's a mystery I haven't been able to solve yet.

I wonder if water made such an impression on me in my visit to Leeds Castle because it seems to have done little else but rain recently. The weather has its advantages though. The parklands around the castle glistened and glowed, like a teenager tossing back freshly washed, shiny, shiny, long hair.

And the sounds. Rushing and tapping and gurgling and ... honking.

Forget the famous queens and the porpoises, it's the water birds that rule Leeds Castle today. I tried to walk sternly past them, but these geese meant business. In fact, given their very obvious sense of entitlement, I wasn't surprised to learn that birds were deliberately introduced into the garden. The most recent 'lady' of Leeds Castle was Olive, Lady Baillie, who loved birds of all kinds, and developed part of the parkland as an ideal environment for waterfowl. She also introduced the black swan, the symbol of the castle, to the United Kingdom, importing them from Australia.

She seems like quite a woman. During her time at Leeds Castle, it was a centre of parties and innovation. As I walked round, I tried to picture some of the guests over the years here... Noel Coward, Errol Flynn, Edward and Mrs Simpson, Douglas Fairbanks and Mary Pickford, and David Niven who would apparently desert his fellow guests to play cards with the servants.

But during the Second World War, like many grand country houses, the Castle opened itself up to other 'guests'. It was used for secret meetings with senior military figures, but continuing the female theme, was mostly a centre for the VADs (Voluntary Aid Detachments). Then, as a military hospital and convalescent home for airmen during the Battle of Britain, some arrived still harnessed to their parachutes. But it was another group of visitors I was interested

A black swan swims serenely in front of the castle

in, the so-called 'guinea pigs' - war burns survivors who had been treated by the pioneering plastic surgeon, Sir Archibald McIndoe, at nearby East Grinstead.

I wondered if it was a coincidence that, although much of the original furniture remains, there are so few mirrors in the castle. Instead, there were windows everywhere. Every room I entered, every corridor I walked down, had windows which drew you to look out to the parkland beyond. Even the 'Gloriette', a Spanish term for a Moorish garden building, encourages you to look into the internal courtyard. It must have been a relief to gaze out to the garden instead of worrying about catching your reflection before there is time to come to terms with the new 'you'.

Since I've been visiting gardens in Kent, I've been interested in how they relate to each other, and the different sets of neighbours (and maybe friends and allies) at different times. In the library at Leeds Castle, there is a copy of Sir Philip Sidney's *Arcadia*, printed in 1638. He was, of course, the owner of nearby Penshurst Place.

Perhaps it was a gift between neighbours, both interested in nature and gardens.

Later, I walked round the maze. On my own, thinking it would be easy. Only 2,400 yews. Bring it on. A stroll in the park. I got lost at the first turn. And then again at the second. My heart started to pound like a cartoon character. I began searching for sticks and things I could wave over the top of the hedges because

Do you dare to go down to the Grotto?

I wasn't sure anyone had seen me go in. I tried to retrace my footsteps and got lost again.

I resorted to deep breathing. Tracking the footsteps in the mud to see which direction they were going.

And then, just like that, I was out. And heading for the grotto as my treat. Two seconds later and I was cursing myself all over again for going in on my own. This is scary wonderful gothic stuff based on Ovid's Metamorphoses, and got me thinking about transformation and identity again, and especially the Second World War pilots who had started the war as beautiful boys and had to learn in these 'loveliest' grounds to look, and be looked at, so differently.

Narcissus

A letter to one of Sir Archibald McIndoe's 'Guinea Pigs'

A work of art, the nurses call you,
the stitching on your cheek as fine
as tapestry. *You'll have me hanging
in the Gloriette,* you play the castle fool,
but the rough stones under your fingers
could be a self-portrait, your hand a brush
paused on your chin before you remember why
the castle's windows are angled for defence:
it's important to keep looking out.
You head to the mirrored lake, reflections
are a maze you tiptoe through to reach
the heart, each glance becomes a needle
until you're sewing a new picture.

The topiary walk at
Mount Ephraim

23 Mount Ephraim, Faversham

There is a quote about writing from the Canadian author, Margaret Atwood. Even if you aren't writing about yourself, she says, you need a 'little bit of blood to make the gingerbread man come alive'. The garden at Mount Ephraim shows how the narrative in a garden can come alive with a 'little bit of blood' too, because it has been owned by the same family for more than three hundred years, and it is full of stories.

As I walked round with the current owner, Sandys Dawes, I asked him what his favourite bit of the garden had been as a child, and he took me straight away to the topiary walk. These aren't the poetic shapes and animals you might expect – I have never before seen a hedge in the shape of a First World War tank, for example, and another is a little chair that Sandys remembers being lifted up to sit in. Yet another looks like a hat, and then there's also a bomber plane. In fact, the avenue is the history of the last three hundred years in bush form. During the Second World War, an elderly pensioner spent the summer trimming the topiary with hand shears and Sandys himself struggled to maintain the yew hedges with electrical clippers. Sandys said he loves to see visiting children run around the topiary avenue now, often stopping to look up in wonder.

Next we crossed a small wooden bench to the rockery where, as a child, Sandys would persuade his sister to try the 'medicine' concoctions he made from plants in the garden. I love how gardens encourage these emotional memory maps. I remember precisely the exact spot in my garden at home where, aged four, I got the shock of my life by smelling mint for the first time. And then there was the corner where my sister and I found an ants' nest, and best of all, the tiny white flowers I discovered under our hedge and thought were stars fallen to earth. When I think back to that garden now, these memories are as much part of the structure as the walls and trees.

I think Mount Ephraim encouraged these thoughts because, although it is open to the public, it still remains a personal garden. During all the time it has been in the Dawes family, it has never been 'professionally' designed and was restored in the 1950s, after a period of wartime neglect when lettuces were grown on the front lawn, by Mary Dawes, Sandys's mother. She looked after the day-to-day running of the gardens and when she died in 2009, her daughter-in-law, Lesley, took on the job.

There's such a unique quality to many of the gardeners I met during these visits. Although much of their gardens are rooted in the past, these gardeners are always looking to the future. What an act of faith, for example, it must have been to plant an Arboretum such as the one at Mount Ephraim when you will never live long enough to see the fully grown trees. It's hard not to feel the presence of these trees now, and wonder how many samples could have been brought over by one of the ships an early ancestor,

A view of the rockery

and Sandys's namesake, would have sent overseas when he made his fortune with The British India Steam Navigation Company, a merchant navy business established in 1856.

And although it was a cold day when I visited, in many ways the light covering of frost was the perfect way to see the rockery, lake and shrubs that recreated an Edwardian ideal landscape. When I looked back at where we had been walking, our footmarks were marked on the frosty grass like a path of Grandmother's lace. They were definitely pointing onwards.

Seeds

Deep in the root ball of the ship
the plant collector is making a nest.

*When I think of plant collectors I think of Joseph Banks. Although not the first (Chinese
botanists were collecting roses more than 5,000 years ago), he might have been the richest.
His second voyage was with Captain James Cook of the Endeavour to record the transit of
Venus across the sky in 1768. It must have been like a trip to space would be nowadays.
Strange to think that there has only been one other pair of transits between then and now.
The next two will be in 2117 and 2125.*

He counts his catch, tucks each seed
in its own hand-labelled box, an ebony
cabinet ticking with paused hearts.

*Anyway, Joseph Banks caused his own sensation by refitting his quarters on the Endeavour
and funding the expedition at a cost of nearly £10,000, nearly three times what the boat
originally cost to build and a sum that would translate into millions today. He was only
twenty five but obviously passionate in his tastes.*

He dreams of growing a fresh desert
one day, of these dried moments
in the old land coming back to life.

*Luckily, Joseph Banks made it home safely and with most of his collection intact. Others
weren't so fortunate. Francis Masson, sent to Grenada by Banks many years later, was
drafted into the local militia to defend against French attack. There he was caught and
imprisoned by the French and lost most of his specimens. He was eventually freed but, on
the way back to Britain, his ship was hit by a hurricane and the remainder of his finds were
destroyed. On another trip he was caught by a French privateer and nearly starved to death
before being transported to New York. Amazingly, he carried on collecting, going to Canada
but froze to death near Montreal.*

His bones ache as he waters his dust,
While on the deck above the sailors sleep,

Or not. Even if the plant collectors faced danger, their conditions were still easier than the crew, many of who would have been pressganged into service. Another collector sent out by Banks was David Nelson, who travelled with William Bligh, captain of the Bounty.

and no one sees how the wooden
mast dances its memory of the wind's
song until, reaching for water, it leans
too far, loses balance.

It's said that the crew mutineered partly because the plants on board were given all the available fresh water. Before the captain and Nelson were left on a desert island, thousands of plants were thrown over board.

White sails,
like baby gowns, christen the sea.

*The clipped yew hedges
at Doddington*

24   Doddington Place Gardens, Near Sittingbourne

Night Grass

Peace is on the horizon,
a green lullaby of waves,

and all you hear is the swell
of sea. Take off your shoes

to feel the land under your feet,
because you don't have to do anything

but surrender to this world,
the dark green of night grass,

a memory of watching stars
cherry-picking from above,

air stroking, trees rocking you,
and for this moment you are safe;

just lean into the path,
the earth will take your weight.

A quick look at the photograph of the giant hedges at Doddington Place may be confirmation enough that this is a garden not just full of atmosphere but one that allows a little personal eccentricity too. Just as gardens should.

The yews were planted before the First World War, and, with eight gardeners then employed, they were clipped formally throughout the inter-war years.

However, like many gardens, the hedges were neglected during the Second World War and allowed to grow into the strange, cloud-like shapes we see today. Luckily for us, they were kept as they were, and now the mile-long hedges are clipped annually in August to September. I loved the story that the ladders used for this are traditional cherry picking ladders, a nice reminder that Kent is a fruit-growing county.

A view over the pond

The Victorian house was originally built for Sir John Croft (of Croft's sherry) around 1860, but has been the home of the Oldfield family for a century now.

It's an intriguing garden to walk around, and it becomes a game to try to spot which bit was inspired by which owner. There's a Wellingtonia Walk, and as those trees were very fashionable to plant in the mid 19th Century, they must have been the pride and joy of Sir John Croft.

And, as I found, they are perfect for a bit of tree hugging. I've noticed there are several differences in how my friends hug a tree. Some simply refuse; others put a hand on the bark rather like shaking hands; still others give a brief hug, almost a shrug that could almost not be noticed. Me? I'm a full on tree hugger and squeezer. Some may even say a bit needy, so trees such as those at Doddington are perfect.

They are so solid that there is no way they will uproot themselves and run away.

Other bits of the garden – such as the rock garden – are distinctly Edwardian and don't invite hippy tree hugging. They were designed by Maud Jeffreys (née Oldfield) who, with her General husband, purchased the house from the Crofts. Apparently, Mrs Jeffreys was so impressed with the view that she made up her mind to live there even before she set foot in the house. Choosing the garden first – there's a woman after my own heart. And looking out over Kent from the garden on a crisp autumn day, I could sympathise completely. Imagine waking up to this view every morning.

And, like most good gardens, Doddington is still evolving. The rock garden was in the process of a 'touch-up' during our visit, and the folly, described by Sir Roy Strong as a 'piece of Hampton Court', was built as a memorial by Richard Oldfield to his first wife, Alexandra, who died in 1995. The mirrored obelisk sundial, a millennium project, is one of the

Looking over the rockery to the countryside beyond

most effective pieces of garden art I'd seen, reflecting back new views of the garden from every angle.

And as a reminder that what really matters for gardeners is their soil, the woodland garden is the result of a discovery, in the 1960s, that there was deep acid loam here. It proved perfect for rhododendrons, azaleas, magnolias and smaller woodland plants now planted there. I'm definitely going to have to go back in May to get the full benefit of this. An added benefit will also be the hundreds of tulips nodding away in the spring garden.

Although Doddington is still a private garden, it has been regularly opened over the last fifty years as part of the National Gardens Scheme. The garden covers ten acres, but there are footpaths through the estates and walkers are actively encouraged. In fact, I was glad of my walk when I could enjoy the home-made cakes in the tea-room with the gusto they deserved.

The mirrored sundial obelisk designed by David Harber

DESCRIBE A TREE FOR SOMEONE WHO HAS NEVER SEEN ONE...

The lime avenue through the centre of Dane John Gardens

25   Dane John Gardens, Canterbury

City parks are an important part of any garden tour because they really do sum up how we make our own private playgrounds in any public space. You only have to visit a crowded park at the height of summer to see how the visitors arrange themselves to create their own spaces. Encroach on these informal boundaries, where a family is having a picnic or a couple reading their newspapers for example, and you will quickly be made to feel as if you've burst into their front rooms.

Dane John Gardens has been used as a public space for centuries, although it wasn't laid out as formal gardens until local dignitary, Alderman James Simmons, donated it to the city in 1790. It wasn't always the pleasant space it is now. Every time I go, I only just manage to resist telling the students, families and visitors sitting on the grass that their 'spot' is where the plague victims might have lain when they were left out in tents to die during the 12th Century so they didn't infect the rest of the town.

My first thought as a creative response to Dane John was to listen in on other people's conversations, so I first walked round the city walls which border one side of the park. Then I climbed the medieval mound, which has looked over Canterbury since the 1st Century AD. and sat tucked away on one of the little seats at the top. Sure enough, people soon forgot about me there, and I jotted down random snippets of conversation:

Overheard in Dane John Gardens

Don't go too near, missy.
I remember. I'm not saying
it was a bargain. That fountain
splashes. I never would.
After 30 years, you'd think.
You're fitter than me. Although
the buildings are in disrepair.
It's my fault. Can you hear me?
I haven't had time to stop.
And do we have time?
Time for tea, I think.

But to be honest, this didn't satisfy any deep sense of the park's history. So I spent a day searching through files at the British National Newspaper archive to find out what had happened here in the past. And the stories I found were richer – and odder – than I could have hoped for.

Such as a visit by 500 French Professors of Gymnastics, who arrived by train and paraded down the High Street before giving an outdoor demonstration of their skills.

And then there was the daring escapade by a balloonist who, to avoid an aborted flight, cut off his basket and hung instead to the hoop as he floated over the park towards the coast. I did hope the Buffs (The Royal East Kent Regiment) had been playing in the bandstand then to give him some extra air.

Ah, but what about the air raid shelters, first used for storage and then as a safe place for people, as Canterbury was badly

The remains of the air raid shelters

bombarded during the Baedeker raids? These were named after the pre-war German travel guide to Britain, which was used by the German Luftwaffe to pick out 'three star' historic buildings and places to bomb. Not surprisingly, Canterbury Cathedral was one of those chosen, and a particular hard night of bombing took place on 1st June 1942, allegedly in response to the bombing of Cologne. Amazingly, the Cathedral itself was not badly hit, although there were rumours of the Archbishop running out to inspect the damage in his pyjamas.

However, the picture-perfect appearance of the park, with its immaculately manicured edges and colour-coordinated flower beds, encouraged me to pick a poignant story about a thirteen-year-old boy who was caught picking two roses every Sunday. He was probably sentenced – because I can't imagine how he would have had the money to pay the fine – to seven days' hard labour.

Flower beds at Dane John Gardens

The Smell of Roses

Kentish Gazette of Tuesday July 9, 1861:
Henry Sheppard, aged 13 years, appeared at the Canterbury Police Court to answer
a complaint for plucking flowers on the previous day. Henry Court, a gardener, de-
posed to seeing the defendant and another boy walking about the beds, and when they
thought they were not observed he saw the defendant pull two roses. The same thing
occurred almost every Sunday and it was necessary to put a stop to it. The Bench
consulted a short time and ultimately decided to fine the boy 10s 1d, or in default of
payment to be imprisoned for seven days hard labour.

I turned a blind eye the first time I caught him stealing the roses. Thought it was probably a gift for some poor mother, was even pleased he was a good boy. But then I saw him the second Sunday, that hat of his tipped to one side, his thumbs tucked into his waistcoat pockets, swaggering as if he hadn't a care in the world. I've tended those roses like they were princesses, you see. Maybe better, and there he was, laughing at me. I shouted, ran after him, but he was too quick. He even waved as he headed off down Castle Row. I was ready for him the third Sunday, but then the park supervisor promenaded by with his wife and I couldn't be seen running. Two roses every Sunday. It wasn't until the fifth Sunday I finally caught up with him. He was with a friend, one as cheeky as him. They even greeted me, a rose each in their hands. 'That's private property,' I told him. 'You'll be done for that.' He stopped laughing then, made some comment about how we were plant lovers, the three of us. Luckily there was a policeman walking by, and I called out before I could be won over by that smile. The boy liked the smell, he told me just before he was taken away. Just sniffing them wasn't enough, he had to dive his whole face in if he was to keep it with him all week. He showed me his hands. He was a twine spinner, he said. That accounted for the skin shredding on his palms. He'd wrapped one rose petal round his little finger. I guess the softness was a comfort. I waited for him after the trial. You can come back to the gardens, I told him, but he shook his head as they took him away. Of course he wasn't going to have the money for the fine, but seven days hard labour. I didn't expect that. He'll lose his job too. And all because he liked the smell of a rose. Call me tender-hearted but I took him one to the prison after the second day. I guess I knew they wouldn't give it to Henry so I wasn't surprised when the guard crushed it in his hand as I watched, like he was squashing the life out of a bird. And enjoying it. I tell myself a job is a job, and any thieving is bad so I shouldn't blame myself, but I can never look at the roses the same way now. Could you?

A view of the Cathedral through the blossom

26 Canterbury Cathedral Gardens

So let's finish where we began. In Canterbury.

When I think of cathedrals, I often picture the buildings and not the gardens around them. But Canterbury Cathedral, although smack bang in the middle of the city, is where many locals take their sandwiches at lunchtimes, even though it can feel sometimes as if the cold wind is determined to blow you back to your offices. I went to the cathedral school at Ely, where we developed the same casualness about the grounds too, a reminder that cathedrals aren't just places to worship or to visit as a tourist, but very often form the living heart of a city. As well as the public grounds at Canterbury, there are five private Canonical gardens and the King's School, which add to the feeling of space. The Canonical Gardens are opened annually for charity – it's well worth looking out for this very special event.

On one of my visits, I was lucky enough to meet one of the gardeners, Peter Dee, whose mischievous sense of humour and obvious love of the garden reminded me all over again that it is people who matter, even with historic buildings. When I told Peter I was the Canterbury Laureate, he joked, 'You're so grand, am I allowed to be speaking to you?' before taking me to see a line of Dante's poetry on a statue, and displaying his own knowledge of poetry by quoting Dante by heart.

This inscription is just one of the poetry extracts to be found in the Cathedral grounds, but I was there to write my own words. I searched for inspiration and was first taken by the plaque near a walnut tree in the Campanile Garden, which stated that a gardener had planted the tree from seed in 1981. He must have cradled the walnut in his hand, never daring to imagine it would grow this big. Then there was a primrose I spotted, which had obviously been deliberately planted by the path in the Memorial gardens. It was such an individual expression of grief amongst the collective memorials that I couldn't stop thinking about who had put it there. What was the story behind the seemingly random pile of rubble which I knew must be significant from its position in the middle of a just-manicured flower bed? How many paths, doorways and passages (even now hidden ones) are there in the Cathedral precincts? Who has used them over the years?

And why had a perfect Crocus Circle been planted in an otherwise plain piece of grass?

Only looking up at the Cathedral did it become clear. The flower circle was exactly the shape and distance of where the Rose Window would land if the tower fell.

But my favourite place to sit in the Cathedral grounds is the herbarium, with places to meditate near the herbs and healing plants which are both hidden and protected by Cathedral walls. So I started writing about two people who had different reasons for seeking comfort from being near the Cathedral. I used the same format as the herb list I'd downloaded from the Cathedral website.

*The Crocus Circle and
the Rose Window*

I imagine this story being read as if each section had been written on a plant label, and it's been designed so you can, if you want, read it any order and make new meanings.

Sanctuary

Primrose
She spends the afternoon sitting against one of the ruined pillars in the herb garden, chatting with the plants. 'We're ladies who lunch,' she tells the mint.

Toadflax
Since the accident, he finds it difficult to meet people's eyes. He comes to the Cathedral to run his hands over the ancient stones, pressing his palms so deep against the sharp edges he draws blood. Only then does he feel better.

Motherwort
She has everything her mother dreamt of for her - farmhouse near Faversham, a rich husband who's hardly there, committees. Only children are missing. She watches the school parties being shown round the Cathedral and likes the naughty ones best. She imagines how good it must feel to take having a child so much for granted that you could get cross.

Horseradish
He'd been driving past two horses in a field full of daisies, laughing at how they galloped just for the joy of it. He saw the flashing lights, of course he did. But he thought he might gallop across the tracks in time. But then the train reared up, and his heart.

Butcher's Broom
Since the hospital visits began, she's stepped over into a different world from her family and friends. After two hours of machines and chemicals, she longs to fill herself up with the scent of these plants. To inhale the life in them.

Feverfew
No, his heart said. So loudly he remembers thinking the driver of the train must have heard it too. Otherwise why would he have looked so scared. Now the sound deafens him, ringing in time to the Cathedral bells. No. No. No.

Foxglove

She lies flat out on the grass, trying to remember the last time she was touched, flesh to flesh. Although they are careful to warm the metal instruments first, even the nurses settle her down with plastic covered hands these days.

Caraway

A lucky escape. That's what the lawyers said when he was told that charges wouldn't be pressed. His medical notes were used as proof that he'd suffered enough. He doesn't drive anymore, but the Cathedral is only a forty-minute walk away. He'd do it barefoot if he could.

Mouse Ear Hawkweed

Kindness comes from unexpected places. Last week as she was walking through the Westgate in the rain, a teenager handed her a black umbrella before walking on. He had probably taken it from a bin because it was broken, but she doesn't care. She smiles every time she uses it.

Dandelion

He hasn't been able to work since his wife – never strong – left him. His only routine is to come daily to the Cathedral. He wishes he could just let go of it all, allow the wind to take him any way it wants.

Marjoram

A routine medical check and it turns out she's dying. She takes courage from all the hot-country herbs she sees around her battling against the Kent frosts. Because maybe she can be surprising too.

Mint

He's been following the plant's trail for weeks. Sees the gardeners try to contain it but the next day, a shoot pops up in the next bed – fragrantly confident of a warm welcome. He imagines the plant parties that take place after dark, roots tangled together deep under the earth.

Rue

If she puts her hands on the soil, she swears she feels the plants vibrating against her skin, letting loose such a cacophony of emotion – sorrow, anger, joy, fear – that it threatens to overwhelm her. But like the prince's kiss, it wakes her up.

Wild Thyme

'Excuse me,' she says, and he looks up, recognising her. The woman who sits over by the pillar. 'I think I know you,' she seems nervous. 'You're always here,' he says. 'You too,' she says.

Cowslip

They're so easy to overlook. Two ordinary people going off to have tea in a nearby café. But then they stop, look back at the scaffolding on the tower. 'I'm scared,' she says. 'Everyone is,' he says. And yet they keep on walking.

Winter

Like the pilgrim divests himself of worldly goods,
the garden's stripped back to a skeleton,

only the vertebrae of paths holds its truest form,
even as trees keep blossom close, buds aching,

it's still the cutting back that matters most,
while through it all the river's artery rolls,

a trust in what lies beneath, snowdrops
rising like lanterns.

Garden Postcards

Why does the idea of a lost garden exert such a pull on us? Because we can make our own maps?

As well as buying the guidebook, looking at the plant labels and following the nature trails, I have learnt to find a quiet spot where I can listen to the gardens I visit. It is amazing how loudly they speak.

Anemone, buckbean, coltsfoot, dock leaf, elder, friar's balsam, gentian, horehound, iris, lavender, marshmallow, nettle, oxeye daisy, parsley, rose hip, sunflower, thyme, violet, witch hazel, yarrow.

My mother was more used to farmland than suburban gardens. I remember watching her watching our garden from the kitchen window, and although it took some time for her to make it hers, it was then hard to entice her back to the house. When she and my father fought over planting plans, she came alive.

I take a pile of seed catalogues to bed and read them like novels. Does this mean I have reached a certain age?

There was only one part of my childhood garden that hadn't been claimed. My friend Kay and I would climb over the wall to make a den there from leftover bricks and branches. We collected up the old bottles and picked weeds for bouquets. When my parents bought this plot later, they made a gate through the wall and said it could be my special garden. But neither Kay nor I went into it for months. It was never just a piece of land, it was the fact that anything could happen there. Now I look back and see the metaphor – teenage girls and a paused garden, both bursting with potential. Once realised, we were inevitably a disappointment.

I get my students to make a timeline of all the houses they have lived in on one side of the page. On the other, they write their spiritual homes – all the objects, accents, people, countries they've only visited briefly, books that feel familiar to them. The difference in the room as they make these two lists is palpable. One woman sighs deeply with every new spiritual home she thinks of.

Lying out on warm grass, I write about cornflowers and the smell of Bromley lemon soap. If I close my eyes, I can see a particular blue, the air is scented with lemon.

A letter from Napoleon about the gardens in his exile in Elba states he does not approve of the proposed cost for turf during October. He believes that the man who is employing three men all month 'on a garden the size of my hand' should be reprimanded.

I could still walk you round my childhood garden. Which map would you like to follow? The actual geographical outline, the emotional one, or the one filled with all the things I would have liked to have happen?

A Sultan of Turkey had to be restrained from spending the country's entire budget on tulips. He would hold tulip parties where guests would come dressed in the colours of particular petals, their way lit by thousands of tortoises with candles on their back. The light was the perfect height to admire the tulip.

In the third map, there's a white horse grazing over by the roses. He was supposed to be there when I opened my curtains on my twelfth birthday, and my thirteenth, fourteenth, and still now, with every birthday, I secretly hope for him.

A postcard on my office wall shows a cartoon of businessmen growing in pots. A remote hand holds a watering can that sprinkles them with, what? Drive, kindness, more money?

We walk round a Japanese-style garden in Hampshire that contains the paper mill that made the first banknotes for the Bank of England. The apple trees there are descendants of the original trees used, as apple wood offers just the right mixture of strength and flexibility for paper money. The apples that now lie on the ground look as if they are made of gold.

If you held a brand new banknote to your nose, would it smell of apples?

My sister associates rosemary with my mother, but I always think of parsley. Why did we never think to ask her which plant she liked best while she was alive? Or maybe it doesn't matter how many versions of each of us exist out there in the world.

Which plant do you like best? Quickly, tell me before it's too late.

Cultured Llama Publishing

hungry for poetry
thirsty for fiction

Cultured Llama was born in a converted stable. This creature of humble birth drank greedily from the creative source of the poets, writers, artists and musicians that visited, and soon the llama fulfilled the destiny of its given name.

Cultured Llama is a publishing house, a multi-arts events promoter and a fundraiser for charity. It aspires to quality from the first creative thought through to the finished product.

www.culturedllama.co.uk

strange fruits
by Maria C. McCarthy

Paperback; 72pp; 203x127mm; 978-0-9568921-0-2; July 2011; Cultured Llama (in association with WordAid.org.uk)

Maria is a poet of remarkable skill, whose work offers surprising glimpses into our 21st-century lives – the 'strange fruits' of our civilisation or lack of it. Shot through with meditations on the past and her heritage as 'an Irish girl, an English woman', *strange fruits* includes poems reflecting on her urban life in a Medway town and as a rural resident in Swale.

Maria writes, and occasionally teaches creative writing, in a shed at the end of her garden.

All profits from the sale of *strange fruits* go to Macmillan Cancer Support, Registered Charity Number 261017.

> Maria McCarthy writes of the poetry process: "There is a quickening early in the day" ('Raising Poems'). A quickening is certainly apparent in these humane poems, which are both natural and skilful, and combine the earthiness and mysteriousness of life. I read *strange fruits* with pleasure, surprise and a sense of recognition.
>
> **Moniza Alvi,** author of *Europa*

Canterbury Tales on a Cockcrow Morning
by Maggie Harris

 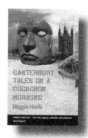

Paperback; 136pp; 203x127mm; 978-0-9568921-6-4; September 2012; Cultured Llama

Maggie Harris brings warmth and humour to her *Canterbury Tales on a Cockcrow Morning* and tops them with a twist of calypso.

Here are pilgrims old and new: Eliot living in 'This Mother Country' for half a century; Samantha learning that country life is not like in the magazines.

There are stories of regret, longing and wanting to belong; a sense of place and displacement resonates throughout.

> Finely tuned to dialogue and shifting registers of speech, Maggie Harris' fast-moving prose is as prismatic as the multi-layered world she evokes. Her Canterbury Tales, sharply observed, are rich with migrant collisions and collusions.
>
> **John Agard,** playwright, poet and children's writer

The Strangest Thankyou
by Richard Thomas

Paperback; 98pp; 203x127mm; 978-0-9568921-5-7; October 2012; Cultured Llama

Richard Thomas's debut poetry collection embraces the magical and the mundane, the exotic and the everyday, the surreal rooted in reality.

Grand poetic themes of love, death and great lives are cut with surprising twists and playful use of language, shape, form and imagery. The poet seeks 'an array of wonder' in "Dig" and spreads his 'riches' throughout *The Strangest Thankyou*.

> He has long been one to watch, and with this strong, diverse collection Richard Thomas is now one to read. And re-read.
>
> **Matt Harvey,** host of Radio 4's *Wondermentalist Cabaret,* and author of *The Hole in the Sum of my Parts* and *Where Earwigs Dare*

Unauthorised Person
by Philip Kane

Paperback; 74pp; 203x127mm; 978-0-9568921-4-0; November 2012; Cultured Llama

Philip Kane describes *Unauthorised Person* as a 'concept album' of individual poems, sequences, and visuals, threaded together by the central motif of the River Medway.

This collection draws together poems written and images collected over 27 years, exploring the psychogeography of the people and urban landscapes of the Medway Towns, where 'chatham high street is paradise enough' ("johnnie writes a quatrain").

> This collection shows a poet whose work has grown in stature to become strong, honest and mature. Yet another voice has emerged from the Medway region that I'm sure will be heard beyond our borders. The pieces here vary in tone, often lyrical, sometimes prosaic but all show a deep rooted humanity and a political (with a small p) sensibility.
>
> **Bill Lewis**

Unexplored Territory
edited by Maria C. McCarthy

Paperback; 112pp; 203x127mm; 978-0-9568921-7-1; November 2012; Cultured Llama

Unexplored Territory is the first anthology from Cultured Llama – poetry and fiction that take a slantwise look at worlds, both real and imagined.

Contributors:

Jenny Cross
Maggie Drury
June English
Maggie Harris
Mark Holihan
Sarah Jenkin
Philip Kane
Luigi Marchini
Maria C. McCarthy
Rosemary McLeish
Gillian Moyes
Bethany W. Pope
Hilda Sheehan
Fiona Sinclair
Jane Stemp
Richard Thomas
Vicky Wilson

A dynamic range of new work by both established and emerging writers, this anthology offers numerous delights.

The themes and preoccupations are wide-ranging. Rooted in close observation, the poems and short fiction concern the 'unexplored territory' of person and place.

A must for anyone who likes good writing.

Nancy Gaffield, author of *Tokaido Road*

The Night My Sister Went to Hollywood
by Hilda Sheehan

Paperback; 82pp; 203x127mm; 978-0-9568921-8-8; March 2013; Cultured Llama

In *The Night My Sister Went To Hollywood* Hilda Sheehan offers poems on love, exhaustion, classic movies, supermarket shopping and seals in the bathtub. Her poems 'bristle with the stuff of life'. Her language is 'vigorous and seductively surreal'. 'What kind of a mother writes poems / anyway, and why?' she asks. A mother of five, Hilda Sheehan is that kind of mother. Read this debut poetry collection now: 'time is running out … Asda will shut soon'.

I was constantly impressed by a sense of voice, and a wonderful voice, clear and absolutely achieved. Throughout ... domestic imagery makes of the kitchen and the household tasks a contemporary epic. The deceptively trivial detail of our daily lives works just as in Dickens, a great collector of trivia, and the pre-Raphaelites, revealing a powerful gift for metaphor. As Coleridge said, metaphor is an important gift of the true poet, and Hilda Sheehan has that gift in abundance.

William Bedford, author of *Collecting Bottle Tops: Selected Poetry 1960–2008*

Notes from a Bright Field
by Rose Cook

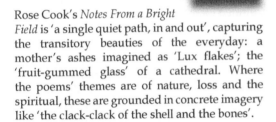

Paperback; 104pp; 203x127mm; 978-0-9568921-9-5; July 2013; Cultured Llama

Rose Cook's *Notes From a Bright Field* is 'a single quiet path, in and out', capturing the transitory beauties of the everyday: a mother's ashes imagined as 'Lux flakes'; the 'fruit-gummed glass' of a cathedral. Where the poems' themes are of nature, loss and the spiritual, these are grounded in concrete imagery like 'the clack-clack of the shell and the bones'.

In their transparency and deceptive simplicity Rose Cook's poems reveal pure and hidden depths in nature, memory and loss, celebrating and questioning the fragility of everyday interactions. These are indeed poems for people 'who juggle [their] lives', insisting in their gratitude that we 'be still sometimes'. To read *Notes From a Bright Field* is to be renewed in body, mind and spirit.

Anthony Wilson, author of *Riddance*

Sounds of the Real World
by Gordon Meade

Paperback; 104pp; 203x127 mm; 978-0-9926485-0-3; August 2013; Cultured Llama

Sounds of the Real World is partly a bestiary, where man and creature are 'separated by nothing but a pane of glass'. The sea is 'a simmer in a pan' throughout, charting the poet's move from his native Scotland to inner city London. Gordon Meade is not just standing and staring at nature; these poems offer social commentary as well as candid reflections on relationships, memory and mortality.

The vicissitudes of tide and weather, the creatures that are his motifs – from the slugs ground under his father's heel to the ghostly gorillas at Heidelberg Zoo – and the vagaries of his own heredity ... all are depicted with clarity and vitality, the familial poems instilling a sense of lurking unease.

Stewart Conn, author of
The Breakfast Room

As Long as it Takes
by Maria C. McCarthy

Paperback; 166pp; 203x127 mm; 978-0-9926485-1-0; February 2014; Cultured Llama

As Long as it Takes gives voice to the lost generation of Irish women who sailed to England to look for work in the middle of the twentieth century. Maura Flaherty and her daughters struggle with identity, belonging, love, sexuality and grief – and dilemmas such as whether to like punk or Elvis.

With no concessions to nostalgia or sentimentality, this deeply moving and beautifully written book, by a second-generation Irish writer, tells the interwoven stories of an immigrant family. Maria C. McCarthy skilfully weaves the historical and cultural significance of Anglo-Irish relations into a half-century of family life.

> Dark, impeccably minimalistic stories about immigrant Irish mothers and their English-born daughters. The mothers belong to the 'lost generation' of Irish workers who emigrated to England in the middle of the last century. They call Ireland 'home' and inflict old-fashioned Catholic morals on their English daughters growing up in a more liberated time and culture. Out of this tension comes a series of stories written from the perspective of several women family members, transcending these painful differences with their courageous humour and absolute refusal to look away. The stories reinforce each other and create memorable echoes, reverberating in the mind long after the book is closed.

Martina Evans, author of *Petrol*

Read individually, these stories might seem modest: each cuts its small piece of cloth and lays it out with truthfulness, understanding and warmth. But characters recur and situations illuminate one another, so that when we read them together we find ourselves inside the story of a whole community of Irish immigrants, suddenly faced, as the protagonists are, with the tellingly displaced expectations and longings of a generation of women and their legacy to the generations that succeeded them. Maria C. McCarthy knows how to tell this complex story, and she tells it with humanity and imagination. The thoughts, speech and actions of her characters make them intensely alive.

Susan Wicks, author of *A Place to Stop*

Lightning Source UK Ltd.
Milton Keynes UK
UKOW06f1120060614

PP1362000001B/1/P

9 780992 648565